INTRODUCTION

Wﾟhat exactly is a ghost? Before I wrote *Ghost Hunter* in 1962, the question might have been an academic one or a controversial one, depending on one's point of view. When the question of haunted houses came up in polite conversation, people were generally split into two uneven groups: the majority, who thought the notion that there were indeed such things as ghosts amusing, if not preposterous; and a tiny but interested minority who believed that that was indeed possible.

Ever since the dawn of mankind, people have believed in ghosts. The fear of the unknown, the certainty that there was something somewhere out there, bigger than life, beyond its pale, and more powerful than anything walking the earth, has persisted throughout the ages. It had its origins in primitive man's thinking. To him, there were good and evil forces at work in nature, both ruled over by supernatural beings, and to some degree capable of being influenced by the attitudes and prayers of man. The fear of death was, of course, one of the strongest human emotions. It is still. Although some belief in survival after physical death has existed from the beginning of time, no one ever cherished the notion of leaving this earth. Thus death represented a menace.

An even greater threat was the return of those known to be dead. In the

French language, ghosts are referred to as *les revenants*—that is to say, the returning ones. To the majority of people, ghosts are those coming back from the realms of the dead to haunt the living for one or another reason. I am still being asked by interviewers why such-and-such a person came back as a ghost. My psychic research and my many books published since 1962 have of course refuted the notion that ghosts are *returnees* from the land of the dead. Every indication drawn from direct interrogation of those who have had experiences of a psychic nature, as well as communications with the so-called "other side of life," has indicated to me that ghosts are not travelers in any sense of the word.

Then what are ghosts—if indeed there *are* such things? To the materialist and the professional skeptic—that is to say, people who do not wish to be disturbed in their belief that death is the end of life as we know it—the notion of ghosts is unacceptable. No matter how much evidence is presented for the reality of the phenomena, they will argue against it and ascribe it to any of several "natural" causes. Either delusion or hallucination must be the explanation, or perhaps a mirage, if not outright trickery on the part of parties unknown. Entire professional groups who deal in the manufacture of illusions have taken it upon themselves to label anything that defies their ability to reproduce it artificially through trickery or manipulation as false or nonexistent. Especially among photographers and magicians, the notion that ghosts exist has never been a popular one. But authentic reports of psychic phenomena along ghostly lines keep coming into reputable report centers such as the various societies for psychic research, or to people who are parapsychologists like myself.

Granted that a certain number of these reports may be due to inaccurate reporting, self-delusion, or other errors of fact, there still remains an impressive number of cases that cannot be explained by any other means than that of extrasensory perception.

In this book I am not telling my readers of legends or unconfirmed sightings, nor of romanticized stories of ghosts that walk only at certain times but at no other. Many such reports have a basis in fact, but unfortunately that basis has never been verified by me or anyone whose word I can accept as reputable. Frequently various tourist organizations pounce upon media reports of ghostly occurrences to build them into tourist-attracting stories. While this is certainly not harmful to anyone—least of all the ghosts if there are real ones on the premises—it does not lend itself to the kind of verifiable, scientific effort I am interested in, nor does it promise a casual visitor to the place the remote possibility of a personal encounter with a phantom even if he is possessed of extrasensory perception.

What exactly is a ghost? In terms of psychic research, as I have defined

Hans Holzer's

HAUNTED
HOUSE
ALBUM

Hans Holzer's

HAUNTED HOUSE ALBUM

Text and Photographs by Hans Holzer
Illustrations by Catherine Buxhoevenden

Dorset Press, *New York*

Photo credits:
Page 23, *Bert Shankland*
Page 91, *Jim Stark*
Pages 183, 184 (top), 185, *Voltava, Vienna*

This edition published by Dorset Press,
a division of Marboro Books Corp.,
by arrangement with the author.
1992 Dorset Press

Printed and bound in the United States of America

ISBN 0-88029-745-X

M 9 8 7 6 5 4 3 2 1

TABLE OF CONTENTS

Hans Holzer's

HAUNTED
HOUSE
ALBUM

them, a ghost appears to be a surviving emotional memory of someone who has died traumatically, and usually tragically, but is unaware of his death. Ghosts, then, in the overwhelming majority, do not realize that they are dead. Those who do know they are "dead," are confused as to where they are, or why they feel not quite as they used to feel. When death occurs unexpectedly or unacceptably, or when a person has lived in a place for a very long time, acquiring certain routine habits and becoming very attached to the premises, sudden, unexpected death may come as a shock. Unwilling to part with the physical world, such human personalities then continue to stay on in the very spot where their tragedy or their emotional attachment had existed prior to physical death.

Ghosts do not travel; they do not follow people home; nor do they appear at more than one place. Nevertheless there are also reliable reports of the apparitions of the dead having indeed traveled and appeared to several people in various locations. Those, however, are not ghosts in the sense I understand the term. They are free spirits, or discarnate entities, who are inhabiting what Dr. Joseph B. Rhine of Duke University has called the "world of the mind." They may be attracted for emotional reasons to one or the other place at a given moment in order to communicate with someone on the earth plane. But a true ghost is unable to make such moves freely. Ghosts by their very nature are not unlike psychotics in the flesh; they are quite unable to understand fully their own predicament. They are kept in place, both in time and space, *by* their emotional ties to the spot. Nothing can pry them loose from it so long as they are reliving over and over again in their minds the events leading to their unhappy deaths.

Very few parapsychologists do anything about these trapped souls. I nearly always do, because I feel it my moral duty to help them out of their predicament, not just study their cases. The method I have developed over the years calls for the presence of a professional trance medium—that is a person who has the ability of slipping in and out of his or her physical body at times. This permits the ghost personality to use the medium's body to express himself.

When the ghost tells his tale of woe, he also relieves the pressure of being trapped in the spot of the haunting. It is a little like psychoanalysis except that the "patient" is not on a visible couch.

As soon as the identity of the haunting personality has been established through questioning by me, the ghost is coaxed into telling of his grievances. Gradually, I explain the true situation to him, that time has passed, that the matter no longer carries as much weight as it once did, and, finally, gently, that he himself is "dead," though very much alive in another dimension, and should go out into it of his own free will.

Sometimes this is difficult for the ghost, as he may be too strongly attached to feelings of guilt or revenge to "let go." But eventually a combination of informative remarks by the parapsychologist and suggestions to call upon the deceased person's family will pry him loose and send him out into the free world of spirit.

Not many individuals have the proper ability or training to be good trance mediums. I have worked with Ethel Johnson Meyers, Sybil Leek, Betty Ritter, Trixie Allingham, and a few others, and I am constantly training young people in this very difficult branch of true mediumship.

The proof of superior mediumship lies only in the results. If the alleged ghost, while possessing the medium's body, can give substantial information about his past, and if that information is checked out by me and found to be substantially correct, then the "channel of communication" has been a good one.

In the majority of published cases, I have been able to prove that the knowledge obtained through a trance medium under my direction was unknown to the psychic person and could not have been obtained except by a qualified researcher such as myself, and even then with considerable effort.

Specific names, dates and situations concerning the life of the ghost have been brought to me in this manner, and there is no doubt in my mind that the information emanated from the so-called ghost. The best mediums serve simply as channels without expressing or even holding explanatory views of their skills, leaving that to the parapsychologist.

Ghosts have never harmed anyone except through fear found within the witness, of his own doing and because of his own ignorance as to what ghosts represent. In the few cases where ghosts have attacked people of flesh and blood, such as the ghostly abbot of Trondheim, it is simply a matter of mistaken identity, where extreme violence at the time of death has left a strong residue of memory in the individual ghost. By and large it is entirely safe to be a ghost hunter, or to become a witness to phenomena of this kind.

In terms of physics, ghosts are electromagnetic fields originally encased in an outer layer called the physical body. At the time of death, that outer layer is dissolved, leaving the inner self free. With the majority of people, this inner self—also referred to as the soul by the church, or the psyche by others—will drift out into the nonphysical world where it is able to move forward or backward in time and space, being motivated by thought and possessed of all earth memories fully intact. Such a free spirit is indeed a development upward, and as rational a human being as he or she was on earth.

Not so with the ghost individual. Here the electromagnetic field is unable to move out into the wider reaches of the nonphysical world, but instead stays captive within the narrow confines of its earthly emotional entanglements. Nevertheless, it is of exactly the same nature as the personality field of those who do not have such problems. It can therefore be photographed, measured as an existing electric charge in the atmosphere, and otherwise dealt with by scientific means.

Science has long realized that all life energies are electric in nature. In my view, human personality is also made up of such energy particles. They are put together differently with each individual, resulting in the great variety of human character, but they are all working the same way—as carriers of personality, thoughts, feelings, and expressions.

Electrical impulses are capable of being recorded and measured. The "presence" of ghosts has already been proven with equipment designed along Geiger-counter lines. But I had always wanted to go one step further and prove these beings pictorially. Psychic photography is the answer. Ever since ordinary wet plates were invented and cameras used, there has also been an interest in photographing the Unseen.

Briefly, the system requires not only a camera and film, or at least light-sensitive photographic paper, but more importantly, the presence in the immediate vicinity of a person with the gift of photographic mediumship. Such an individual is able to act as catalyst between the thought-projection originating in the mind of the spirit or ghost and the light-sensitive film or paper. There is, in my view, some substance in the body of such a medium that makes the process of psychic photography possible. Certain glands secrete this substance only when the medium is "in operating condition," so to speak. I have worked with John Myers, Dr. Von Salza, Ethel Meyers, Betty Ritter—and other gifted individuals in this specific field. I myself have on occasion been able to get psychic photographs when there was someone with that special talent in my vicinity. The light-sensitive surface of film or paper seems to become coated with invisible but very sensitive psychic matter which in turn is capable of recording thought imprints from beyond the world of matter.

Naturally, all ordinary explanations must always be taken into consideration. Faulty equipment, light leaks, double exposure, faulty development or printing, reflections, refractions, and, finally, delusions of the viewer are all possible. Two examples of my own results are herewith reproduced to illustrate the point. After all the above-mentioned possible explanations had been weighed and found to be unsatisfactory, only the parapsychological version remained.

Both photographs were taken by me with a perfect Zeiss camera, called the Super Ikonta B, with fresh Agfa Record Isopan film, and on firm surfaces. Both are time exposures of about two seconds, and the development and printing was done by first-rate people.

In the case of the three cowled monks seen at Winchester Cathedral, there is a history of persecutions during the reign of Henry VIII. Ghostly monks have from time to time been observed in the nave of the great church.

In the second case, that of a haunted house in Hollywood, California, a teen-ager was murdered during a wild party not too long ago, and disturbances have plagued the owners ever since. A partially visible figure slightly above the bed, dubbed by me "the girl in the negligée," cannot be accounted for by any "ordinary" explanation, such as window curtains, light reflection, and so on.

As for the photographs of actual ghosts, I have published them in *Psychic Photography—Threshold of a New Science*, and others elsewhere have also come forward with photographs taken in so-called haunted houses under conditions excluding fraud, double exposure, faulty equipment or development, and any other alternate explanation. Among these are a recent photograph taken at Newby church in Yorkshire, England, revealing a cowled figure of a monk standing to the right of the altar. The picture clearly shows a semitransparent figure with a whitish face and two holes for eyes but no recognizable features. In this particular instance, the photograph has been attested by an English photographic laboratory. The fact that photographs can be produced artificially to duplicate what has transpired under test conditions free of fakery does in no way affect the genuine facts. One must never forget that the possibility of fakery is not the same as the certainty of falsehood. It merely means that the expert must be fully cognizant of the possibilities and must devise his test conditions in such a way as to exclude any and all fraud. This has been done in all cases of ghost photographs published by me, and with such other authenticated pictures as the Newby church ghost monk, and the celebrated "lady on the staircase"— actually the brown lady of Raynham Hall, Yorkshire, England, which *Country Gentleman* and *Life* published in 1937.

In his chapter on ghosts, Douglas Hill in *Man, Myth, and Magic*, takes all alternate hypotheses one by one and examines them. Having done so, he states, "None of these explanations is wholly satisfactory, for none seems applicable to the whole range of ghost lore." Try as man might, ghosts can't be explained away, nor will they disappear. They continue to appear frequently all over the world, to young and old, rich and poor, in old houses and in new houses, on airports and in streets, and wherever tragedy strikes man. For ghosts are indeed nothing more or nothing less than a human being trapped by special circumstances in this world while already being of the next. Or, to put it another way, human beings whose spirit is unable to leave the earthly surroundings because of unfinished business or emotional entanglements.

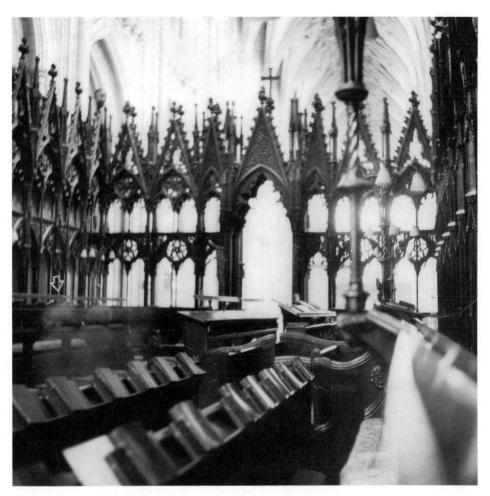

The three cowled monks at Winchester Cathedral.

Ghosts, then, are very real, and the range of those who may at one time or another observe them is wide indeed. Anyone who sees or hears a ghostly phenomenon is by that very fact psychic. You do not have to be a professional medium to see a ghost, but you do have to be possessed of more than average ESP abilities to tune in on the refined "vibrations" or electromagnetic field that the human personality represents after it leaves the physical body. There are of course millions of such people in the world today, most of them not even aware of their particular talent.

Ghosts attract the believer and nonbeliever alike, even if the attitude is different. I cosponsor summer tours of European legendary castles with Swissair, and the people who come on these very special journeys need not be dyed-in-the-wool spiritualists by any means. Quite a few former skeptics, however, have returned somewhat shaken by what they have experienced in haunted places. You never know *who* turns out to be psychic!

This book lists some of the most interesting and most accessible haunted houses around the world. These are houses where ghosts have been observed by one or more competent observers and where the likelihood of a reoccurrence of the phenomena still exists. There is no telling whether a casual visitor might have an experience or not. Ghosts do not appear on command, and even spending the night in a haunted house might produce nothing more than a stiff neck or the sniffles. Then again, one might walk into a haunted house, unaware of that fact, and have an experience quite unexpectedly. Such is the thrill, and the uncertainty, of following in a ghost hunter's footsteps—one can never be sure what might transpire.

In seeking out some of the houses described in the following pages, keep in mind that a relaxed, open-minded attitude toward the phenomena is helpful. Patience is a must. What might not happen on the first visit might very well occur on a subsequent trip. There is no hard and fast rule concerning the success one seeks in having a ghostly experience. There is only a reasonable likelihood of experiencing something in a haunted house if one is oneself somewhat psychic. If one is actually psychic to a high degree, then the chances are that one will at least feel something of the unseen inhabitant of the place. Whenever this is possible, take photographs using black and white film and time exposure, and something that the naked eye does not see might very well show up on your film.

And if you who read these lines are a complete skeptic and consider visiting haunted houses just a lark, remember an old quotation of uncertain origin, "I don't believe in ghosts, but I'm sure as hell scared stiff of 'em!"

But even if you do not encounter ghosts or have a psychic experience in the houses described here, you will find them fascinating places. As an adventure in historical research, haunted houses have no equal.

UNITED STATES
OF AMERICA

CALIFORNIA

WHALEY HOUSE,
SAN DIEGO

The Whaley House, situated in a part of San Diego called Old Town, was originally built in 1857 as a two-story mansion by Thomas Whaley, a San Diego pioneer. It stands at the corner of San Diego Avenue and Harney Street and is now being kept as a museum under the guidance of June Reading; it can be visited during ordinary daylight hours. As a matter of fact, thousands of people visit it every year—not because it is haunted, but because it is an outstanding example of early American architecture. Since I published the amazing accounts of the hauntings at the Whaley House in my book *Ghosts of the Golden West*, even more visitors have come, and the added enticement of perhaps meeting up with a ghost has added to the attractions of the old mansion.

There are two stories connected by a staircase. Downstairs there is a parlor, a music room, a library, and in the annex, to the left of the entrance, there used to be the County Courthouse. At least one of the hauntings is connected with the courtroom. Upstairs there are four bedrooms, tastefully furnished in the period during which the Whaley House was at its zenith—that is to say, between 1860 and 1890. The house was restored by a group of history-minded citizens in 1956. If it were not for them, there would now not be any Whaley House.

Numerous witnesses, both visitors to the house and those serving as part-time guides or volunteers, have seen ghosts here. These include the figure of a woman in the courtroom, sounds of footsteps in various parts of the house, windows opening by themselves in the upper part of the house despite the fact that strong bolts had been installed and thus they could only be opened by someone on the inside; the figure of a man in a frock coat and pantaloons standing at the top of the stairs, organ music being played in the courtroom where there is in fact an organ although at the time no one was near it and the cover closed; even a ghost dog has been seen scurrying down the hall toward the dining room. There is a black rocking chair upstairs that moves of its own volition at times, as if someone were sitting in it. A woman dressed in a green plaid gingham dress has been seen seated in one of the bedrooms upstairs. Smells include perfume and the smell of cigars. There is also a child ghost present, which has been observed by a number of people working in the house, and a baby has been heard crying. Strange lights, cool breezes, and cold spots have added to the general atmosphere of haunting permeating the entire house. It is probably one of the most actively haunted mansions in the world today.

Despite my thorough investigation with the help of Sybil Leek, arranged for by television personality Regis Philbin, some of the apparitions have remained, and reports of continuing disturbances are still coming in to me. As far as I could ascertain through the trance session with Sybil Leek, the ghosts include the builder of the house, Thomas Whaley, who had a just grievance against the city of San Diego which probably has kept him tied to the house. He had put money into certain alterations so that he could sell the house to the county to be used as a courthouse. However, his contract was never executed and he was left "holding the bag." Sybil also pinpointed a child ghost correctly, age twelve, by the name of Annabelle, and named the lady ghost upstairs correctly as Anna Lannay, Thomas Whaley's wife.

It is wise to ask for a guided tour or at the very least check in with Mrs. June Reading to be sure that the ghostly spots are properly pointed out. Since there are so many of them, one can hardly avoid at least one of the several hauntings at the Whaley House.

THE SPECTER OF NOB HILL, SAN FRANCISCO

On California Street, not far from the Fairmont Hotel, where the cable car stops, there is an intersection flanked by some of the oldest houses in San Francisco. It is here that the ghost of Flora Sommerton walks. Mrs. Gwen Hinzie has seen her as recently as 1962. She was riding up to California Street in a cable car in the company of a friend. Both ladies, looking out the window, noticed a strange girl walking up the street beside the cable car, wearing what appeared to be an odd dress for the time of day. The dress Mrs. Hinzie described as a kind of ballgown, and what was even more remarkable was the fact that the stranger seemed to walk right through people ahead of her. Others have noticed the lovely young girl seemingly walking straight ahead, as if she was trying to get away from something or someone down the hill.

The case concerned a San Francisco debutante, Flora Sommerton. A few hours before her scheduled debut, eighteen-year-old Flora disappeared from her mansion on Nob Hill, causing one of the major scandals of the year 1876. Her reason was that she did not care to marry the young man her parents had picked out for her. The girl was never found despite a huge reward offered for her return.

Ever since her disappearance, rumors circulated that she had been seen here or there, but all of them turned out to be false. For the most part, these were feeble attempts at getting money from Flora's parents. However, as the years went by and the girl did not turn up, the family built a wall of indifference around themselves and Flora was no longer discussed. The reward was withdrawn. No one who wanted to remain on good terms with the Sommertons dared mention Flora or to ask if anything new about her had turned up.

The parents eventually accepted the medical theory that Flora's mind had snapped under the pressure of prewedding excitement. It was better to believe this version than to admit to themselves the real cause of Flora's panic. The man they had wanted her to marry was simply not the man she wanted. Afraid to face her parents in rebellion, she did the only thing she was capable of under the circumstances: she ran away. She did not even wait to change clothes, running up hill in a ballgown. Truly Flora's action was not premeditated but sudden, and in panic.

When the parents died, even the rumors of Flora's reappearance died out. It was not until much later that her name became once again newsworthy in her native city.

Eventually, Flora died broke and ill in 1926, in a flophouse hotel in Butte, Montana. When found, she was dressed in a white ballgown of the 1880s. It was that same ballgown she was wearing when Mrs. Hinzie saw her ghost walking up Nob Hill with a determined look.

I cannot promise that in today's traffic anyone will notice the unusually clad young lady, but it is just possible that in the still of night and with great patience, a sensitive individual might feel her presence in the area. If you will slowly walk up and down the hill, starting at California Street, perhaps you will be one of the lucky few.

THE STAGECOACH INN, THOUSAND OAKS

Not far from Ventura, at Thousand Oaks, a few yards back from the main road, stands an old stagecoach inn, now run as a museum; between 1952 and 1965, while in the process of being restored to its original appearance, it also served as a gift shop under the direction of a Mr. and Mrs. MacIntyre who had sensed the presence of a female ghost in the structure.

The house has nineteen rooms and an imposing frontage with columns running from the floor to the roof. There is a balcony in the central portion, and all windows have shutters, in the manner of the middle nineteenth century. Surrounded by trees until a few years ago, it has been moved recently to a new position to make room for the main road running through here. Nevertheless, its grandeur has not been affected by the move.

During the stagecoach days, bandits were active in this area. The inn had been erected because of the Butterfield Mail route, which was to have gone through the Conejo Valley on the way to St. Louis. The Civil War halted this plan, and the routing was changed to go through the Santa Clara Valley.

I investigated the stagecoach inn with Mrs. Gwen Hinzie and Sybil Leek. Up the stairs to the left of the staircase Sybil noticed one of the particularly haunted rooms. She felt that a man named Pierre Devon was some-

how connected with the building. Since the structure was still in a state of disrepair, with building activities going on all around us, the task of walking up the stairs was not only a difficult one but also somewhat dangerous, for we could not be sure that the wooden structure would not collapse from our weight. We stepped very gingerly. Sybil seemed to know just where to turn as if she had been there before. Eventually we wound up in a little room to the left of the stairwell. It must have been one of the smaller rooms, a "single" in today's terms.

Sybil complained of being cold all over. The man had been killed in that room, she insisted, sometime between 1882 and 1889.

She did not connect with the female ghost. However, several people living in the area have reported the presence of a tall stranger who could only be seen out of the corner of an eye, never for long. Pungent odors, perfume of a particularly heavy kind, also seem to waft in and out of the structure.

Like inns in general, this one may have more undiscovered ghosts hanging on to the spot. Life in nineteenth-century wayside inns did not compare favorably to the Hilton. Some people going to these stagecoach inns for a night's rest never woke up to see another day.

Thousand Oaks is about an hour and a half from Los Angeles on the Ventura Freeway. No special permission to visit is needed.

THE HAUNTED BARN, THOUSAND OAKS

Not far from Thousand Oaks stands a simple wooden church called Missionary Baptist Church. It is situated on a small bluff overlooking the freeway access road. This church is actually an old dairy barn remodeled, first into a theatre, and later, when the theatre people left, into the present church. (The original owner, a Mr. Goebel, sold it to the Conejo Valley Players, an amateur theatrical group.) There is a large door in front, and a smaller one in the rear, by which one can now gain access to the church. There is also an attic, but the attic is so low that no one can possibly stand up in it. This is of importance, since the observed hauntings seem to have emanated from that attic. Footsteps have been heard overhead by some of the Conejo Valley Players, when there was positively no one overhead. If there had been anyone standing in the attic, he would have had to have been no more than three feet tall. No flesh and blood person can stand up in the attic. What was once the stage of the Conejo Valley Players is now the area of the altar. The minister of the Baptist church does not take kindly to psychic phenomena, so a visitor must make his own arrangements or simply walk into the church—for worship, as it were—and garner such psychic impressions as he or she can without causing any stir.

The phenomena consisted mainly of a man's footsteps. Someone was

pacing up and down in the attic. At first, no one paid any attention to it, trying to pretend the noise was not real. Eventually, however, members of the audience kept asking what the strange goings-on over their heads meant. Was there another auditorium there? Sometimes it sounded as if heavy objects such as furniture were being moved around. There was of course nothing of that kind in the attic.

One young girl, who had not been a member of the troupe for long, became almost hysterical and insisted that someone had been murdered in the building. Two ladies with psychic leanings could never enter the structure without immediately getting cold, clammy feelings. These feelings mounted and turned into terror when they attempted to go up into the attic, and, on hands and knees, look around for the cause of the strange noises.

Hurriedly, they went down again. The noises continued, not only at night during actual performances, but even in the afternoons during rehearsals or casual visits.

Sybil Leek stuck her head into the attic immediately when we entered the barn. To her, that was the place of the haunting, although I had not told her anything whatever about the problem. Serious-faced, she walked about the barn for a while, again poked her head into the attic, standing on a few steps leading up to it and then shook her head. She explained the young man who had been murdered here would not leave. There had been a love triangle, and he had been the victim of a stabbing. The fact that the barn was now a church had made no impression on him. He keeps pacing up and down.

DISTRICT OF COLUMBIA

THE OCTAGON, WASHINGTON

One of the prime assets of the nation's capital is the fact that many of its buildings were individually designed and are therefore unique. In larger cities such as New York or Los Angeles, you do not encounter this kind of architectural attractiveness. One of the best-known monuments to Washington's past is the Octagon, the seat of the American Institute of Architects, and a museum.

Originally built by Colonel John Tayloe in 1800 as his town house, the mansion stands in one of the most fashionable parts of Washington. The plot upon which it is built, at the corner of New York Avenue and Eighteenth Street, was originally surrounded by empty land, but today it forms the center of several avenues of mansions and expensive town houses. There are three stories, it stands at the corner of two streets, and the building itself is octagon-shaped. The downstairs part boasts a magnificent rotunda, whence a staircase leads to the second and third stories. This staircase is the center of ghostly activities. Most of the reported phenomena took place on the second floor landing near the bannister, or on the third floor, which is not open to visitors. Just recently the entire building was overhauled once again, to make it more attractive to the continuing influx of tourists who come not to look for a ghost but to visit a museum of renown and a historical landmark, for

 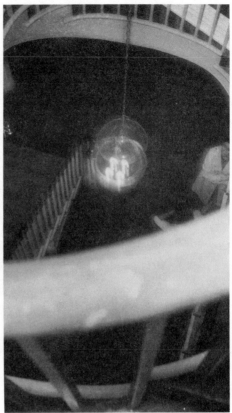

some of the greatest names in American history are connected with the Octagon.

Even while it was being constructed, General Washington spent time here, and during the British occupation of the capital and the subsequent construction of the White House, the Octagon served as temporary White House to President Madison and his wife, Dolley, and he signed the peace treaty with Britain here in 1815. After the death of Mrs. John Tayloe in 1855, the building passed into other hands. At first it was used as a school for girls, but as the immediate neighborhood deteriorated for a time, it became a slum building. It was rescued from that ignoble fate in 1899 when the American Institute of Architects took it over.

Ghostly phenomena have been reported as far back as the middle nineteenth century. They have included reports of footsteps, the wailing of a female voice, and other uncanny signs of a human presence in the old mansion. There is a long list of rational, uncommitted observers who have experienced inexplicable things at the Octagon. One of the superintendents, Alric H. Clay, has on several occasions found the lights put on again after he had turned the switches off, and the doors wide open, after he had just locked them securely. Footsteps of both a man and a woman have been heard re-

peatedly, especially on the third and second floors. A carpet at the bottom of the main staircase keeps flinging itself back when there is no one in the building. The chandeliers swing of their own volition at times. These phenomena may very well still occur since no one has made any attempt to exorcise the resident ghosts. From all indications, and a recent investigation with medium Ethel Johnson Meyers, I know that there are at least two entities still present at the Octagon.

One is the daughter of Colonel Tayloe, who committed suicide by jumping from the second-floor landing. Her body was found just where the carpet keeps flinging itself back of its own volition. The other must be the distraught father, Colonel Tayloe himself. It was his refusal to accept his daughter's choice of a husband that drove her to an untimely death. However, there may very well be also a third ghost at the Octagon. During the British period, a young officer pursued one of the American servant girls, who preferred to jump to her death rather than give in to his demands. We do not have her name, but visitors often report someone standing behind them on the upper floors. Those were the servants' quarters. The Tayloe girls would more likely be felt further below.

The Octagon is generally open to visitors, whether or not they are interested in ghosts. As a matter of fact, the American Institute of Architects is not especially fond of the notion that there might be other things among its exhibits than old manuscripts and artifacts. But I have no doubt that the hauntings at the Octagon continue.

MARYLAND

THE HAUNTED FRIGATE
CONSTELLATION,
BALTIMORE

Tied up at the pier in Baltimore and open to the public as a kind of floating museum, is the proud U.S.F. *Constellation*, once the flagship of the American Navy. Built in 1797 as the first man-of-war of the United States fleet, the ship was still in commission as late as World War II. Part of its superstructure has recently been restored, and the timbers are only partially the original wood, but otherwise nothing has been changed. This is important since the hauntings would not continue if most or all of the original material had been replaced.

Congress tried to decommission the U.S.F. *Constellation* several times and to pass her name on to a newer ship. But something would always happen to prevent this, or the new carrier of the name *Constellation* would become the victim of accidents. Gradually, however, the old ship outlived her usefulness, and, despite her heroic past, found herself forgotten at Newport, Rhode Island, where she was slowly but surely falling into disrepair. Franklin Delano Roosevelt resurrected her from this ignominious position and recommissioned her as the flagship of the U.S. Atlantic fleet in 1940, but funds to restore her were lacking, and the ship was towed to Boston. In 1953, a private committee of Baltimore citizens collected sufficient funds to get the ship home to Baltimore and restore her to her pristine glory. This has only just been done, and anyone visiting the *Constellation* at her Baltimore pier makes

a small contribution to the maintenance of the old ship. Visitors are admitted, although no one is permitted to sleep aboard. Ever since I published the account of the ghostly happenings aboard the ship, people, out of curiosity, wanted to spend the night aboard. Since the ship is all wood, fire hazards exist, and the committee cannot permit anyone to stay on after dark. Frankly, I wouldn't if I were just a curious person, because two of the three resident ghosts aboard the U.S.F. *Constellation* are certainly still there.

Those interested in the complete details of the hauntings might read about them in my book *Window to the Past*, or talk to the curator, Donald Stewart of Baltimore. The first ghost is an old sailor who keeps appearing to visitors wearing the uniform of bygone days. With the help of medium Sybil Leek I was able to pinpoint more accurately the other two haunting personalities. They are associated with the so-called orlop deck below the main deck, and the area near where the gun emplacements used to be. The two haunting entities were closely associated with each other. One was the ship's captain Thomas Truxtun. The other was a watch who had fallen asleep on duty and in the cruel manner of the times had been condemned to death by the captain. Death was administered to the unfortunate one by being strapped to a gun and blown to bits. The executed sailor is the other ghost, and Captain Truxtun's own feelings of guilt perhaps caused him to remain aboard.

Sybil Leek also felt the presence of a cabin boy who somehow had come to grief aboard ship, but she described that event as having happened at a later time, around 1822, whereas the events involving Captain Truxtun took place between 1795 and 1802. As for the man blown to bits, the unfortunate sailor's name was Neil Harvey, and he has been seen at various times by visitors to the ship who knew nothing whatsoever about the ghostly traditions attached to it.

A visit to the U.S.F. *Constellation* is a must if you are ever in the area. There is no need for an advance appointment, nor is it necessary to hide one's interest in the ghostly happenings aboard.

THE SURRATT TAVERN,
CLINTON

Thirteen miles south of Washington, in a small town now called Clinton but once known as Surrattville, stands an eighteenth-century building nowadays used as a museum. Mary Surratt ran it as an inn at the time when the area was far enough removed from Washington to serve as a way station to those traveling south from the nation's capital. When business fell off, however, Mrs. Surratt leased the eighteenth-century tavern to John Lloyd and moved to Washington where she ran a boardinghouse on H Street between Sixth and Seventh streets. But she remained on close and friendly relations with her successor at the tavern at Surrattville, so that it was possible for her son John Surratt to use it as an occasional meeting place with his friends. These friends included John Wilkes Booth, and the meetings eventually led to the plot to assassinate President Lincoln.

After the murder, Booth escaped on horseback and made straight for the tavern. By prearrangement, he and an associate hid the guns they had with them in a cache in the floor of the tavern. Shortly after, he and the associate, David Herald, split up, and John Wilkes Booth continued his journey despite a broken foot. Eventually, he was discovered hiding at Garrett's barn and shot there.

The connection between Booth and the tavern was no longer public

knowledge as the years went by. Some local people in the village might have remembered it, but the outside world had lost interest. At one time the structure was acquired by John's brother the actor Edwin Booth, it appears. In the 1950s it passed into the hands of a local businessman named B. K. Miller. By now the village was known as Clinton, since the Surrattville name had been changed shortly after the infamous trial of Mary Surratt.

Mr. Miller still owns the building although he was trying to sell it to an historical association at the time of my visit, so that it might be preserved as a landmark.

During his ownership in the 1950s and 1960s, he allowed a relative to live at the house. The lady occupied the downstairs part. Downstairs there are a large front room, a narrow hallway, and a smaller bedroom; a large room to the rear of the building is the one where Booth hid the guns in the floor. Upstairs there are bedrooms on both sides of the landing.

The hauntings observed here include the figure of a woman, thought to be the restless spirit of Mary Surratt herself, whose home this had been at one time. Strange men have been observed sitting on the back stairs when there was no one but the occupants of the house around. Muffled voices of a group of men talking in excited tones have also been reported, and seem to

indicate that at the very least an imprint from the past has been preserved at the Surratt Tavern. Many meetings of the conspirators had taken place in the downstairs part of the building, and when I brought Sybil Leek to the tavern she immediately pointed out the site of the meetings, the place where guns had been hidden, and, in trance, established communication with the former owner of the tavern Edwin Booth himself.

Although the building is now a museum and open to visitors, one should first obtain permission from Mr. Miller, at Miller's Supermarket, in Clinton, Maryland. Clinton itself is less than an hour's drive from downtown Washington. As far as I know there is no fee attached to a visit at Surratt Tavern. At the time when I made my investigation, Mr. Miller had thought to sell the building to a museum or an historical trust, and by the time this appears in print, it may well have changed hands.

NEW HAMPSHIRE

OCEAN-BORN MARY'S HOUSE, HENNIKER

If you ask the present owners of the Ocean-born Mary House, Mr. and Mrs. David Russell, whether they have a ghost, they will vehemently deny it. They have had some bad experiences. On Halloween some youngsters mistake a haunting legend in a beautiful old house for license to misbehave and throw rocks. So the Russells will deny that any ghostly manifestations have ever taken place at their house. They prefer to call it a museum, and allow the public to visit it most of the time for a small entrance fee.

But I have conducted several investigations—invited by the Russells—because of the ghostly goings-on. I have worked with a local medium and with Sybil Leek, and there is no doubt that the surviving spirit of Mary Wallace, whose home this once was, is still present in the structure.

Mary is the ocean-born child who was befriended by a pirate, named Don Pedro. Later in life he helped her build this house, and in turn she permitted him to spend his old age as her pensioner. Unfortunately for Don Pedro, so the story goes, one of his men who had been disgruntled caught up with him, and in the ensuing fight Don Pedro was killed. Allegedly his body lies underneath the fireplace, but there is no proof since the fireplace has never been dug up.

The place came to my attention when a local amateur medium by the name of L. A. asked my assistance in dealing with the phenomena she had encountered at the house. During a routine visit as a tourist, she had found herself practically taken over by the spirit of Mary Wallace who demanded to be heard through her. Frightened, she fled home to a Boston suburb. That night she awoke and, without being able to resist, drove her car all the way up to New Hampshire, still in her nightclothes.

I brought Mrs. A. back to Ocean-born Mary's with me, in the daytime and wearing street clothes, and in trance Mary Wallace manifested. The gist of her communication through the medium was a concern for the proper maintenance of the old house and an almost playful desire to be acknowledged and recognized.

Subsequent to this visit I also drove up with Sybil Leek and attempted another trance session. Sybil managed to bring through a servant girl who had apparently met with foul play or was involved in it. At any rate, she must be the third resident ghost, in addition to Mary Wallace and her pirate friend.

There was also talk of a buried treasure somewhere on the grounds. The directions were quite explicit and after Sybil came out of trance we all went

out and looked for the treasure underneath the stones behind the house. We did not dig, of course, and treasures have a way of staying underground, especially after two hundred and fifty years.

While there may be some speculation about the reality of the hidden treasure and possibly of the continued residence "in spirit" of the pirate, there is substantial evidence that the house is haunted by a woman greatly resembling the original owner.

A number of people have seen the tall, stately figure of Mary Wallace peering out of an upstairs window of the two-story structure. It was her favorite place, and from the description given there is no doubt that those who saw the figure were indeed seeing the ghost of Mary Wallace.

On one occasion, her intervention saved the house from burning to the ground. A heater had caught fire, but was smothered by unseen hands. The ghost has been described by one who saw her as "a lovely lady in her thirties with auburn-colored hair, smiling rather intensely and thoughtfully."

On one occasion, two state troopers saw her walking down the road leading up to the house, wearing a Colonial-type costume, and a casual visitor to the house was shown around by a tall lady at a time when the Russells were away. Only later did this visitor realize that it had been Mary Wallace who had been so hospitable.

The house can be reached by car from Boston. It is worth a visit.

NEW JERSEY

RINGWOOD MANOR

About an hour's drive from New York City, in northern New Jersey not far from Saddle River, stands Ringwood Manor. The house was built on land purchased by the Ogden family in 1740 and was originally connected with an iron-smelting furnace. In this area iron ore was found in large quantities, and in the late Colonial period smelting of iron ore was a major business here. The fortunes that built Ringwood Manor were made of iron.

The main portion of the house dates back to 1762. Eventually it became the property of Robert Erskine, the geographer of George Washington. The local iron business soared to great heights as a result of the Revolutionary War, and the profits enabled Martin Ryerson, the owner of Ringwood Manor, to rebuild it completely in 1807, tearing down the original old house.

However, after the iron business fell off in the 1830s, the house was sold to Peter Cooper and eventually passed to his son-in-law Abram S. Hewitt, one-time mayor of New York. Mrs. Hewitt changed the rather drab house into a mansion of fifty-one rooms, very much in the style of the early Victorian Era. She moved various smaller buildings, already existing on the grounds, next to the main house, thereby giving it a somewhat offbeat appearance. In 1936, Erskine Hewitt left the estate to the state of New Jersey,

and the mansion is now a museum which can be visited daily for a small fee. Not too many visitors come, however, since Ringwood Manor does not merit the kind of attention some of the better-publicized national shrines attract.

I visited Ringwood Manor in the company of Ethel Johnson Meyers to follow up on persistent reports of hauntings in the old mansion. One of the chief witnesses to the uncanny goings-on was the superintendent of the manor, Alexander Waldron. He had heard footsteps when there was no one about, footsteps of two different people, indicating two entities. Doors that had been shut at night were found standing wide open in the morning when no one human could have done it. The feeling of "presences" in various parts of the house persisted. There is a local tradition that the ghost of Robert Erskine walks about with a lantern, but there is no evidence to substantiate this legend.

As a result of my investigation and Mrs. Meyers' trance, I discovered that the restless one—at least, one of them—was a so-called Jackson White, living at the house at one time. The Jackson Whites are said to be a strange mixture of Negro and Indian and white. They are descendants of runaway slaves who settled in parts of New Jersey in the nineteenth century and lived among the hill folk.

The center of the hauntings seems to be what was once the area of Mrs. Erskine's bedroom, but all along the corridors both upstairs and downstairs there are spots where a sensitive person might experience chills or cold clammy feelings. I made contact with the surviving personality of Mrs. Erskine, as well as the unhappy servant whose name was Jeremiah. In the end not too much could be accomplished with either entity, as they insisted on remaining where they were and in the state of partial detachment from reality that had turned them into ghosts to begin with.

But Jeremiah complained bitterly about his mistress who had allegedly mistreated him. The lady of the manor merely told us to get off her property!

Remote though Ringwood Manor is from the life of New York City, it is worth a visit, and the possibility of experiencing something out of the ordinary is still quite strong.

NEW YORK

CAFE BIZARRE,
NEW YORK CITY

The Cafe Bizarre on West Third Street, near Sullivan Street, is in a very well preserved three-story building dating back to pre-Revolutionary times. It was remodeled in the early nineteenth century, and it is probably one of the oldest buildings in Greenwich Village.

The building was part of the stables of Aaron Burr, but prior to that, it was owned by a British Colonial family. Burr used it well into the 1830s, after which its history is unclear.

The ground floor portion of the building is a kind of duplex loft, properly decorated for a night club with a bizarre motif. The rear section of this room has been the center of ghostly manifestations. I have investigated the place on two occasions. A ghostly apparition of what may very well have been Aaron Burr, from the description, has appeared to a number of people working at the Cafe Bizarre. A waiter and the owner's wife, Mrs. Renée Allman, have described the intense-looking man in a white ruffled shirt with piercing black eyes and short beard. A visitor to the Cafe Bizarre, a young girl by the name of Alice McDermott, also had a psychic experience in which she saw the same figure. As a result of my two investigations with mediums Ethel Johnson and later Sybil Leek, Mr. Burr's restless personality was freed from the place where so many emotional memories had kept him captive.

The trance interrogation was particularly dramatic. At first, the entity speaking through Mrs. Leek evaded my questions concerning its identity. At no time did "he" admit to being the late Aaron Burr. That was hardly necessary. Under questioning, the spirit spoke of conditions only Burr would have been familiar with in these surroundings. For instance, at the very outset, the spirit cried out for Theo, asking me to find her for him. Theo had been Burr's only daughter, whom he had lost early in life. She was aboard a ship that never reached her destination and to this day we don't know whether the ship sank in a storm or fell victim to piracy.

Theo is a very unusual name. Only the Burr family has used it for its women during the period under investigation.

Another reason why I found the identity of the spirit convincing involved Burr's exile in France. Under questioning (and without prodding or leading questions on my part), the entity spoke of spending time in France. He spoke of wearing a beard and having to hide from his enemies. When I insisted that he tell me his name, he mentioned the name Arnot. Later research disclosed that Burr did have to hide from Napoleon's police, that he had a short beard when he returned from his French exile, and that the cover name he had used while in France was indeed Arnot. None of this could have been known to Mrs. Leek, or, for that matter, to me. The Cafe is still being operated as a nightclub and can be visited evenings without difficulty.

CLINTON COURT, NEW YORK CITY

Hell's Kitchen is not one of the best neighborhoods of Manhattan. The houses lining the streets generally do not show much charm or artistic invention. Thus it must come as a great surprise to the casual visitor when he passes by the facade of number 420 West 46th Street, goes through a narrow lane closed off by an iron gate, and finds himself in a courtyard of great beauty and charm. Across the courtyard is another building, number 422½ West 46th Street. This is Clinton Court, named after Governor George Clinton whose carriage house it once was. The ground itself was at one time used as a Potter's Field, the cemetery for the poor and for the executed. Consequently there are "presences" here in various spots, remainders from New York's past, when this area was fairly far "uptown."

When the British ruled New York, one of those buried here was a certain character known locally as "Old Moor," a sailor executed for mutiny.

His ghost was the first phantom seen at this place. In the 1820s, when the house was still used as carriage house for the estate of Governor Clinton and his family, Old Moor would appear and frighten people. One day he frightened the wife of a coachman, who fell down the winding stairs to her death. These very stairs, leading from the upper story to the ground, still exist, although a second staircase, farther to the rear, has since disappeared.

The coachman's wife became ghost number two.

The ghostly legend of the house was so well known that the Clinton children played a private little game called "Ghosts." One day, one of the Clinton children, frightened by a real apparition, stumbled and fell to her death, becoming ghost number three. This child ghost was seen by the late Ruth Shaw, an artist who had rented the downstairs portion of the carriage house some years ago. All of the hauntings are confined to that part of the building. The front, giving on to 46th Street, has never been affected.

I have held several investigations at this address, including one with Ethel Johnson Meyers and another with Sybil Leek. I have also made a television film about it. Through Sybil I met the ghost of a Colonial officer named Walker at 422½ West 46th Street. Enough personal data was received and checked out in regimental records to prove that such a man existed and that, at any rate, the medium could not have known about it. He died in a duel.

While it is not difficult to walk into the courtyard of Clinton Court, as the house is still called, getting access to the two apartments is another matter. They are privately owned and do not look for visitors—especially not those who come for the ghosts rather than the flesh and blood people. Today the house is divided between two tenants. The family of Leo Herbert, property man for David Merrick, lives upstairs, and the Nearys have the downstairs portion. But since some of the phenomena have actually occurred outside the building, on the winding staircase and in the courtyard itself, it is entirely possible that a sensitive individual might experience *something* outside the apartments. I suggest that one go there at dusk and experience the quietness of the courtyard in contrast to the surrounding street noises. In particular, I suggest a walk up and down those winding stairs. Who knows which one of the four resident ghosts one might encounter?

A CONFEDERATE GHOST
IN NEW YORK CITY

Probably the most protracted investigation I have ever undertaken, and the most evidential case for the existence of ghosts, was the one that took me to number 226 Fifth Avenue in New York City. I published the complete results in my first book *Ghost Hunter*, after spending five months and seventeen separate sessions investigating this haunting.

Two twenty-six Fifth Avenue was at one time an elegant town residence, later turned into an apartment house. At the time of my investigation in 1953, the top floor apartment, a duplex, belonged to a Captain Davis, an explorer who was abroad much of the time.

Seven years later, the apartment house was shut down for repairs. For about two or three years it stood empty and began to look rather dismal. The area around this building is strictly commercial, and I thought it was only a matter of time before the building itself would be torn down to make room for a new skyscraper. Imagine my surprise when I recently passed the building. Far from being torn down, it has been reconditioned, and though it is no longer an elegant town house, and has commercial tenants on each floor, at least its basic structure has been maintained, the outside cleaned up, and the stairs still lead up to the top floor apartment that was once haunted.

Tenants of the top floor apartment prior to Captain Davis included

Richard Harding Davis and the actor Richard Mansfield. We have no record whether they were disturbed by the resident ghost or not, but Captain Davis was. Thanks to an introduction by the late *Daily News* columnist Danton Walker, I was able to enter the case in conjunction with a group of fellow students then working at the headquarters of the Association for Research and Enlightenment. As a result of my long investigation, I learned of a Confederate hero officer crossing lines in the midst of war in order to see his mistress.

General Samuel Edward McGowan, of McGowan's Brigade, is historically fully documented. There is of course no mention of his ghostly captivity at 226 Fifth Avenue New York. To the official historian, he died later and lies buried in his hometown cemetery at Abbeyville, South Carolina. But the material coming through medium Ethel Johnson Meyers was so evidential and filled with detailed knowledge of the Civil War that I do not doubt in the least the harrowing account of McGowan's adventures in New York City.

Separation and war being what it was, the general's lady love, Mignon Guychone, of French Creole stock, had apparently taken up with another gentleman, named Walter. Despite the fact that she loved the general and vice versa, and that they had had a baby from their union, a conflict arose. Walter showed up unexpectedly and strangled general McGowan. In order not to be charged with murder, however, he made it appear like suicide, and hanged the lifeless body of the Southern gentleman from the rafters in the little attic.

The most urgent need of the ghost—once he could communicate with us—was to set the record straight as to his suicide. Committing suicide was alien to the traditions of a gentleman officer, and McGowan was at great pains to explain that it was murder and not self-inflicted death. General McGowan certainly is not there any longer, for he has communicated with me on numerous occasions afterward from various places, something a true ghost cannot do, since ghosts are tied to the place where their tragedy has occurred until such time as they are freed from their emotional entanglements. But those wishing to visit this most famous of all my haunted houses can probably do so without even asking permission. The house is open during business hours, and though the top floor tenant may be somewhat surprised to have a stranger ring his bell or walk into his door, I leave it to the ingenuity and good sense of my readers to make up a suitable excuse.

THE GHOST AT THE PUPPETEER'S THEATRE, NEW YORK CITY

Frank Paris is a world-famous puppeteer, but he has also taught his art at Columbia University. He lives at number 12 Gay Street, Greenwich Village, New York City. The house is a four-story building of the kind that was popular around the year 1800. It is in excellent condition and is one of the jewels of the area. Gay Street is just around the corner from bustling Sixth Avenue, and it sometimes is hard to find unless one knows how to get there.

Frank Paris has turned the basement into a workshop for his puppet theatre. There, too, at various times he has given performances with his favorite puppets. The second story has been turned into a duplex apartment for himself and his assistant. It is filled with odd sculpture, antiques, paintings, and other witnesses of his vast and curious tastes. There are gargoyles, devils' masks, Javanese dancers, reflecting his fertile artistic talent.

The house remained unaltered until 1924, when a new section was added, covering a garden which used to exist in back of the house. At one time, Mayor Jimmie Walker owned this house and used it for one of his lady loves. Prior to Mr. Paris's ownership it belonged to real estate broker Mary Ellen Strunsky.

The owner, his friends, and even guests have experienced the sensation

of unseen entities walking up and down the stairs at night, and on at least one occasion, a man in evening dress appeared at the door, smiling politely and then dissolving into thin air before the very eyes of reputable witnesses.

I first brought medium Betty Ritter to the house, and she made contact with a restless entity dating back to the prohibition era. She had no idea of the connection between Mayor Walker's "friend" and the house. Later, Ethel Meyers brought through a French diplomat who complained he had been tortured here but had held on to his "secrets." There is evidence the house did exist at the time of the Revolutionary War. Not long ago, medium Shawn Robbins came with me to the house for another visit, which was televised. Again, she made contact with a tortured soul who had died violently for holding on to "something." As for the gentleman in evening clothes, no one knows who he is.

Frank Paris's house is not open to the public, but it is worth a try to coax him into letting you see his workshop if you are at all interested in puppets. And if you mention that you like ghosts, quite possibly Mr. Paris will open the door to you too.

JUNE HAVOC'S TOWN HOUSE, NEW YORK CITY

At 428 West 44th Street, near Ninth Avenue, Manhattan, stands an impressive town house built more than a hundred years ago. Originally the property of the Rodenberg family, the four-story stone house passed into the possession of a certain man named Payne. Using the original building plans to restore the Victorian house, he made no changes in the structure and tried to follow all the intentions when he restored the house of the original architect in the 1950s. Between 1962 and 1969 the building was the property of the well-known stage and screen actress June Havoc. She rented the upper floors to various tenants, but she herself used the downstairs apartment.

Miss Havoc's former apartment is reached by a staircase to the parlor floor. For some strange reason, tenants never stayed very long in that ground-floor apartment, but Miss Havoc paid no special attention at the time. Before long, however, she noticed a number of strange things. Tapping noises at various times of day and night kept her from sleeping or concentrating on her work. They were not the kind of noises one could explain away by natural causes. Miss Havoc made sure of that by having experts come to the house and examine steampipes, flooring, and walls. The main area of activity seemed to be the kitchen and the rear section of the house.

I held two seances at the house with medium Sybil Leek. On the first occasion, an entity calling herself Lucy Ryan made a noisy entrance by demanding something to eat in a loud voice not at all like Sybil's own.

I immediately questioned the spirit and discovered that she had starved to death during a fever epidemic. She claimed to have lived in the year 1792. At that time, the house had of course not yet been built and the land was simply part of the surrounding estate without any human dwelling on it.

When I demanded to know why Lucy was still around, she explained she was waiting for her soldier by the name of Alfred. Regimental records are available to check into soldiers' identities. I asked Lucy, through Sybil Leek, who had commanded the regiment in which Alfred had served.

"Napier" came a quick reply. The following day we checked this out and found that Colonel Napier was the commanding officer of a regiment stationed in the grounds of Governor Clinton's estate. The land on which Miss Havoc's house stands was part of that estate in 1792. Also, a fever epidemic in fact occurred at that time and Colonel Napier himself had been shipped back to England in very poor condition.

We freed Lucy from the house and vice versa. In a second seance we tried to get rid of the soldier. Unfortunately, he was of sterner stuff. Complaints of noisy phenomena keep coming to me, so I must assume dear Alfred has not quite left.

Miss Havoc has since sold the house, ghost and all. How the current owners feel about visitors I can only guess.

June Havoc's Town House

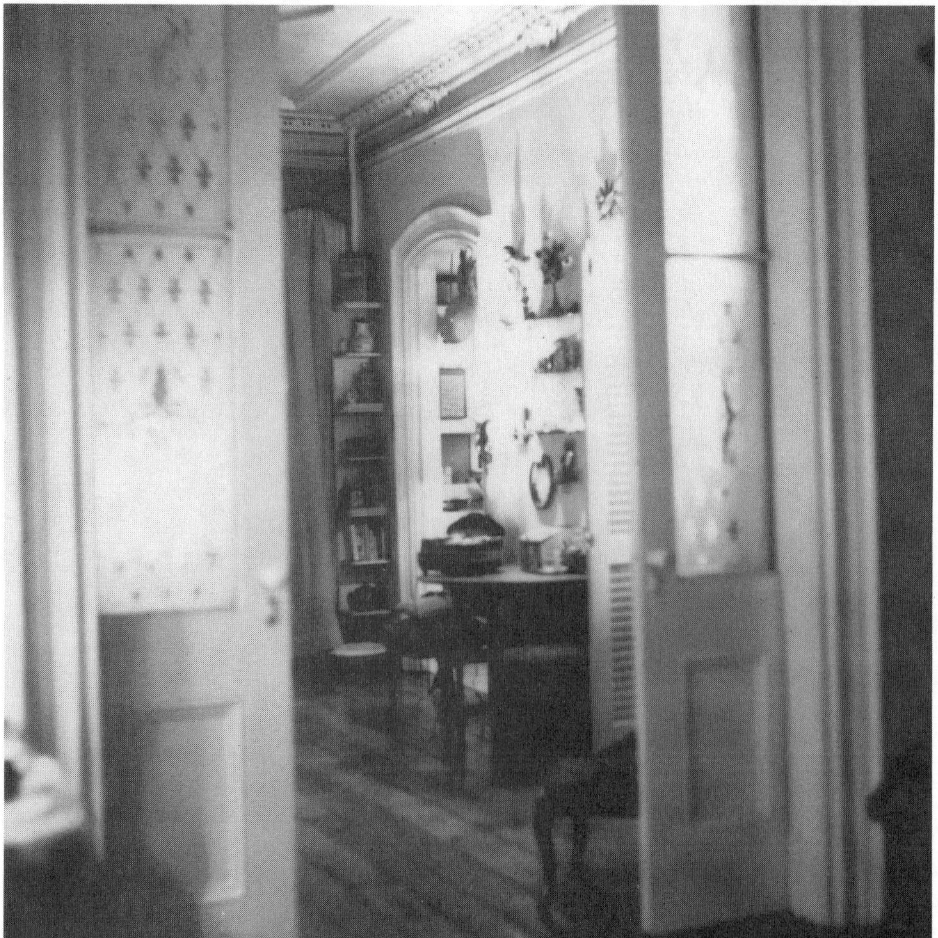

THE MORRIS-JUMEL MANSION, NEW YORK CITY

At the corner of Edgecombe Avenue and 160th Street in Manhattan there stands a magnificent mansion built in the grand manner of the eighteenth century. It would be more at home in the south, but in New York City it seems even more splendid. This is as it should be, as the building is located on the highest spot of Manhattan, originally called Harlem Heights.

English-born Colonel Roger Morris built the mansion, and in 1776 during the Revolutionary War it was taken over by American troops. General Washington made it his headquarters during his New York campaigns. Later the British moved in, and General Sir Henry Clinton stayed at the mansion. After that, the career of the building was a somewhat checkered one. At one point it was an ordinary tavern called Calumet Hall. One day in 1810 a French wine merchant named Stephen Jumel and his ambitious wife passed by and decided to buy the place which included thirty-five acres of land surrounding it. Madame Jumel refurbished and renovated the place, and it became one of the jewels of New York City.

There are four stories and a basement, and the principal areas of psychic interest are the second and third floors, as well as the balcony, which can be seen from a distance. It was on that balcony on January 19, 1964, that a small group of schoolchildren saw the ghost of Madame Jumel, which in turn

triggered the first of my several investigations into the hauntings at the Morris-Jumel Mansion.

Up one flight in what used to be Madame Jumel's bedroom, I held a seance in which Stephen Jumel complained bitterly about being murdered by his wife. The one-time Vice President of the United States Aaron Burr, who married the widow Jumel and spent some time at the mansion, also has been felt by people—although I doubt that he was ever a resident ghost there. There was also a young servant girl who got herself involved with one of the family and who committed suicide by jumping out the window. It is possible that she is one of the ghosts being observed on the top floor. After my second and third visits to the mansion, I should expect Stephen Jumel to be no longer in evidence. However, Madame herself and the servant girl may very well still roam the corridors. There is also a soldier who died there, and who has been seen by a teacher and a group of children during a recent visit.

The Morris-Jumel Mansion may be visited during the daytime at certain hours. It is maintained as a museum by the Daughters of the American Revolution. The curator is Mrs. Emma Bingay Campbell. She knows all about the ghosts. She is also a very gracious lady.

THE OLD MERCHANT'S HOUSE, NEW YORK CITY

At 29 East 4th Street stands one of few remaining brownstone houses which has preserved its original appearance completely. It was built in 1830. Untouched by the decay of the surrounding area, the house managed to survive the great changes of recent years.

The house became the property of Seabury Tredwell, a wealthy merchant in the hardware business, as soon as it was completed by its builder. It was very convenient for his business.

The house is a Federal style building with windows opening onto Fourth Street. Originally a lovely garden surrounded the house, but today the garden is gone. The entrance is particularly imposing with two columns in classical style, at the top of a few steps and wrought-iron lanterns adorning the door. There are three floors topped by an attic, and there is also a basement.

Inside, the furniture is still of that period. There was a banister by Duncan Phyfe, and a fine staircase leading to the upper three stories. The downstairs was filled with fine furniture, some of it also by Duncan Phyfe, a rectangular piano which is still there, and in showcases along the walls one finds some of the costumes left behind.

The ghostly phenomena in the house center around Tredwell's three daughters, Phoebe, Sarah, and Gertrude. According to tradition, Mr. Tredwell did not take kindly to any suitor who seemed to want to marry his daughters for their financial status. This material served as the background for Henry James's famed *Washington Square*, which much later became a motion picture called *The Heiress*, and for a story of mine in *Gothic Ghosts*.

The main manifestations occurred in the kitchen on the ground floor level in the rear of the house. But what used to be Gertrude's bedroom upstairs also has a presence in it from time to time. The ghost is that of a small elegant woman dressed in the finery of the middle nineteenth century. That this is Gertrude herself is very likely, since according to my psychic friend

Ethel Johnson Meyers it was she who died tragically here. There had been an unwanted baby, followed by disapproval of her actions by her family. How much of this can be proven objectively is doubtful, but a presence has been observed in the Old Merchant's House by several reliable witnesses, and no attempt has been made to exorcise her since after all this was her home.

One need not dwell upon the ghostly manifestations, as far as the curator is concerned, since she may not be aware of them. But I suggest a visit to the kitchen area, the back bedroom upstairs, and Gertrude's front bedroom. It contains a small canopied bed, which, according to at least one witness, is haunted.

One eerie story told about the Old Merchant's House concerns the fireplace on the third floor. Allegedly it cannot be photographed. I tried my luck with a very good camera while a professional photographer who was with me at the time also photographed the fireplace. Although the fireplace did appear on both pictures, there is a strange white area around it that cannot be accounted for.

The house is open to visitors at certain hours since it is now a museum maintained by a private group.

ST. MARK'S IN-THE-BOUWERIE, NEW YORK CITY

There really isn't any reason why churches should not also be haunted at times, but somehow the idea of holy ground harboring restless souls does not occur to the average person. Nevertheless, there are a respectable number of such edifices around the world. One of the most colorful ones is the church of St. Mark's in downtown New York City, standing at the corner of Second Avenue and Tenth Street. This area has lately become hippie land, but is reasonably safe in the daytime.

The church itself was built in 1799 on the site of an earlier chapel going back to Peter Stuyvesant and the year 1660. The governor himself is buried in the crypt, which can be seen. The last member of the Stuyvesant family died in 1953, and the crypt was sealed.

Built along neoclassical lines, the church stands in lonely majesty in a garden plot which serves in part as cemetery. This is surrounded by a cast-iron fence, and it seems like an oasis amid the somber-looking utilitarian apartment houses and shops. The church is open in the daytime and one need not obtain permission from anyone to visit it. Although not all rectors feel the same way about ghostly apparitions at their church, my witnesses were all respectable, sane people.

There were two or possibly three ghosts at St. Mark's, and for all I know,

they are still there since no attempt to exorcise them has been made. One is a woman parishioner who appears in the middle of the nave in the central aisle. Another entity has on occasion shown up on the balcony close to the magnificent organ. The ghostly woman has also been observed closer to the entrance door in the rear of the building. Finally, there are the sounds of a man walking with a cane, and it has been thought that this indicates Peter Stuyvesant himself—Father Knickerbocker of the legend—who has a wooden leg and did indeed walk with a cane. It is possible that his death might not have been entirely final for this restless soul. The woman ghost, however, is still in evidence and has been observed as recently as two or three years ago.

THE HAUNTED RECTORY, POUGHKEEPSIE

During my work with the late Bishop James Pike, I got to know the Christ Church rectory at Poughkeepsie pretty well. In 1947 Pike was offered the position of rector, and he spent several years there. Christ Church is a large, beautiful, almost modern Episcopal church. The altar with its candles indicates what are generally called "high church" attitudes, that is, closer to catholicism. The outside of the church has remained turn-of-the-century, and so has the rectory attached immediately to the church itself. There is also a small library between rectory and church, which is one of the centers of the psychic experiences reported by Bishop Pike.

I asked permission of the rector of Christ Church to visit what used to be Bishop Pike's church, and in July of 1968 I took medium Ethel Johnson Meyers there. She relived practically the entire incident Bishop Pike had reported to me privately earlier.

What had occurred during the two and a half years of James Pike's residency at Poughkeepsie was not unusual as hauntings go. To him it seemed merely puzzling, and he made no attempt to follow up on it in the way I did when I brought Mrs. Meyers to the scene. Pike had taken over his position at Poughkeepsie, replacing an elderly rector with diametrically opposed views in church matters to his own. The former rector had died shortly afterward.

Pike soon found that his candles were being blown out, that doors shut of their own volition, and that objects overhead would move—or seemingly move—when in fact they did not. All the noises and disturbances did not particularly upset Bishop Pike. However, on one occasion he found himself faced with a bat, flying about madly in the library. Knowing that there was no way in or out of the library except by the door he had just opened, he immediately closed the door again and went to look for an instrument with which to capture the bat. When he returned and cautiously opened the door to the library, the bat had disappeared. There is no possible way by which the animal could have escaped.

In 1969 I took Ethel Meyers to the church. Contact was made with the surviving spirit of Pike's predecessor, both in the area of the high altar and the library. He spoke of his "errors" concerning religious matters and proved his identity beyond doubt.

Those wishing to visit Poughkeepsie can do so freely, although the rector may not be too keen to discuss psychic phenomena.

THE CEDARS,
RYE

I have spent much time investigating a Victorian manor house called The Cedars, in Rye, New York, belonging to Mr. and Mrs. John Smythe. Mrs. Smythe is better known as Molly Guion, the celebrated portrait painter. The house is a sprawling, mid-nineteenth century manor house standing on a bluff overlooking the New Haven Railroad. It was built around 1860 by a Jared B. Peck, and rises to four floors. There is a wide porch around it on the ground level, and the house itself stands under tall trees protecting it from the road and giving the entire estate a feeling of remoteness despite the fact that the grounds are not very large.

Downstairs there is a huge living room, filled with fine antiques tastefully matched to the period the house itself represents. In addition, there is a sitting room and a kitchen. The ghostly apparition has been seen near the kitchen, as well as on the upper stories.

The second floor contains many smaller rooms. A winding stairway leads to the third floor. Here the rooms are even smaller, since evidently that part of the house was once used as the servants' quarters. There is a sharply angled stairway leading to the attic, closed off by a wooden door. This door has been heard to open and slam shut by itself many times. The attic is Molly Guion's studio. Here she does her work, uninterrupted if possible by both visitors and ghosts. There is also a small bedroom on the attic floor. Mr. Smythe slept in it once and reported footsteps he could not explain on rational grounds.

The phenomena include opening noises of the front door, swinging of the chain when no one was about, and, above all, the movement of heavy objects by their own volition. On one occasion, a carving knife took off in the well-lit kitchen and flung itself at the feet of Mr. and Mrs. Smythe, as if to call attention to someone's presence. On another occasion, an ashtray flew from its place to land slowly on the floor of one of the upstairs bedrooms.

I have held a number of seances at The Cedars, both with Mrs. Meyers and with Sybil Leek. As a result of my investigations, I learned that there are present two different entities—perhaps three. The door-slamming ghost may be that of a former owner, who spent her last remaining years shut up in one of the small upstairs bedrooms. Perhaps she was put there by her family and resented her confinement. At any rate, there are markings on the door of one of the small bedrooms on the third floor indicating that a heavy lock must have been in place at one time.

The second entity whose presence was felt at the house goes back to the early eighteenth century and connects with an earlier house standing on the same spot. A fire is said to have consumed that earlier building, and the entity still recalls the horror of being burned.

Finally, there is a young woman who died tragically at the house in this century and whose presence may account for some of the continuing phenomena. Her signature and face appeared unexpectedly on a frame of a television film made by a crew I sent to Rye, New York, as part of a series of news programs dealing with the occult a short time ago.

There is no doubt that the ghost population of The Cedars has been reduced somewhat due to my visits, but enough remains to give the present owners food for thought.

The house is located on Barberry Lane in Rye, New York; it is privately owned and not open to visitors. However, correspondence with Mrs. John Smythe might conceivably yield some results, if a visitor has a valid reason and not mere idle curiosity. Miss Guion is, as I have said, a professional portrait painter, and anyone wishing to have his portrait painted in her studio upstairs might very well find the sitting not quite as restful as imagined. At any rate, that is what happened to one of Molly's professional models, who was posing nude one day. Thinking that she and the painter were the only ones in the house at the time, she was surprised to find herself face to face with a woman she did not recognize. It was particularly upsetting, since the stranger disappeared almost immediately without benefit of door.

Whether this was the ghost of Mrs. W., the former owner of the house, or the young woman who appeared on film, or the girl who burned to death in the eighteenth century is hard to say. But it was nobody of flesh and blood.

NORTH CAROLINA

THE GHOSTLY MACO LIGHT, WILMINGTON

Not all ghosts or hauntings are tied to buildings. There are haunted crossroads, haunted airports, and even haunted railroad crossings. One of the most famous of all such phenomena still exists at the railroad crossing near Maco, North Carolina, twelve miles west of Wilmington on the Atlantic Coast Line Railroad. Ever since 1867, an itinerant light has been observed by hundreds upon hundreds of people in the area, which could not be explained on natural grounds. Despite attempts by scientists to explain the light as part of swamp gas, reflected automobile headlights, or other natural origins, these so-called explanations have not really answered the question.

In 1964 I made a thorough investigation of the entire phenomenon, and in the course of it interviewed dozens of actual witnesses who had observed the light. There were several among them who had not only seen a light approach along the tracks where no light should be, but had actually, on getting closer, observed that the light was inside an old railroad lantern; and some had even heard the sound of an approaching train close by. The consensus seems to be that a ghostly personality appears at the Maco trestle holding a railroad lantern aloft as if to warn someone or something. This fits in with the tradition that a certain Joe Baldwin was behind the haunting.

Baldwin was a conductor on what was then called the Wilmington,

Manchester and Augusta Railroad, and he was riding in the end coach of a train one night in 1867. The coach somehow left the train and Baldwin grabbed a lantern in an effort to signal a passenger train which was following close behind. Unfortunately, the engineer of the train did not see the signal and a crash was the result. The only one to lose his life in the crash was Joe Baldwin himself, who was decapitated. The signal lantern was later found a distance from the track. There is no question in my mind that the surviving spirit of Joe Baldwin—who, incidentally, is buried in a Roman Catholic cemetery close by the tracks—is still trying to discharge what he considers his solemn duty. Unfortunately he is not aware of the fact that no train is following him any longer.

Those wishing to watch for the ghostly light at Maco, North Carolina, can do so freely, but must exercise patience. Also, there are a considerable number of tourists always in the area, who come for the same reason. Nevertheless, the percentage of those who have seen the ghostly lights is amazingly large. Those wishing additional information about the area should contact the Southeastern North Carolina Beach Association, Wilmington, North Carolina.

PENNSYLVANIA

THE HAUNTED CHURCH, MILLVALE

About an hour's drive from Pittsburgh, in the small town of Millvale, hard by the Allegheny River, stands an imposing stone church built at the turn of the last century. Positioned as it is on a bluff looking down toward the river, it seems somewhat out of place for so small a town as Millvale. Attached to the building is a school and rectory, and there is an air of clean efficiency about the entire complex. This is a Roman Catholic church, and the priests are all of Yugoslav background. Thus there is a peculiarity about the ritual, about the atmosphere inside the church, and about the men who serve here. The church is very large, and the altar is framed by original paintings in the Yugoslav style. They are the work of Maxim Hvatka, the celebrated Yugoslav artist who worked in the early part of this century and who died a few years ago. Near the altar there was a large eternal light —that is to say, an enclosed candle protected from drafts or other interference. This is important, since much of the phenomenon centers in this area and includes the blowing out of the eternal light by unknown causes.

Although the administrators of the church do not exactly cherish the notion that they have a ghost, there have been a number of witnesses who have seen a figure pass by the altar. The painter Hvatka himself saw the ghostly apparition while working on his frescoes. Chills, which could not be

accounted for, were also noted in the immediate area of the eternal light.

There is nothing concerning the present-day church that would account for the apparition of a figure at the altar. However, prior to the erection of the present church a wooden church had stood on the same spot. It was Father Ranzinger who had built the wooden church, and who had devoted most of his life to that church and its flock. One night, the wooden church went up in flames. Father Ranzinger's lifework was destroyed. I suspect that it is his ghost that has been seen.

Ghosts are an embarrassment in many Catholic eyes. When the priests realized the purpose of my visit, they tried to hide the facts from me. However, it was not long until Father X, as he insisted on being called, admitted to having had psychic experiences all his life, including ghostly ones. Since both he and the painter had been the principal witnesses to the phenomena, the two men must have been psychic, something a painter can admit but not a priest, perhaps.

Louis Adamic, an agnostic author, was the first one to publish anything about a ghost here, prior to my visit and investigation.

Nothing whatever has been done to release the ghost—whoever he might be—so that visitors to Millvale might conceivably still experience something uncanny or even run across the ghost at the altar if things are right.

VIRGINIA

CASTLE HILL

Not far from Charlottesville, in the open countryside, is the magnificent estate and mansion of Castle Hill, one of the historical highlights of the area.

The main portion of the house was built by Dr. Thomas Walker in 1765, but additions were made in 1820. The original portion was made of wood while the additions were of brick. These later changes undertaken under the direction of the new owner, Senator William Cabell Rives, gave Castle Hill its majestic appearance. Senator Rives had been American ambassador to France and was much influenced in his tastes by French architecture. This is clear when one sees the entrance hall with its twelve-foot ceilings and the large garden laid out in the traditional French manner.

On the ground floor, to the rear, there is a suite of rooms which has a decidedly feminine flavor. This is not surprising since they were the private quarters of a later owner, Amélie Rives, an author and poetess whose body lies buried in the family plot on the grounds.

In this suite there is a bedroom called the pink bedroom, which is the center of ghostly activities. Whenever guests have been assigned this room to sleep in, they invariably complain of disturbances during the night. Writer Julian Green, a firm skeptic, left the next morning in great hurry. Amélie

Rives herself spoke of a strange perfume in the room, which did not match any of her own scents. The ghostly manifestations go back a long time, but no one knows exactly who is attached to the room.

From the testimony of various guests, however, it appears that the ghost is a woman, not very old, rather pretty, and at times playful. Her intentions seem to be to frighten people using the room. Curiously, however, a few guests have slept in it without being aroused by uncanny noises or footsteps. Legend has it that those the lady ghost likes may sleep peacefully in "her" bedroom, while those she does not like must be frightened out of their wits.

During the Revolutionary War, British Banastre Tarleton and his troops occupied Castle Hill. The then owner, Dr. Walker, served them breakfast on June 4, 1781, and in the course of his hospitality delayed them as long as he could so that Jefferson, then in nearby Charlottesville, could make good his escape from the British. Whether or not one of the ladies played any significant part in this delaying action is not known, but I suspect that there is involvement of this kind connected with the appearance of the ghostly lady at Castle Hill.

Today the estate is the property of Colonel Clark Lawrence. It is not open to visitors.

CANADA

THE HAUNTED MYNAH BIRD, TORONTO

The Mynah Bird is an unusual nightclub in the Yorkville district of Toronto, an artistic neighborhood known for its unusual attractions. The old house is narrow and has two stories and an attic, or third story, if you wish. The Mynah Bird nowadays has so-called skin shows, and occasional "adult movies." Colin Kerr is the owner of this emporium, which is no worse —in fact, much better—than most striptease or sex-exploitation-oriented night-clubs in the United States. The atmosphere is clean, alcohol is not served, and the audiences are small. The main attractions are a series of solo dance performances by seminude girls, a session in body painting (with the customers getting into the act), and, since the haunting was discovered, an occasional seance. The latter smacks of commercialism and is not to be taken too seriously.

The psychic goings-on started when Kerr changed the club's policy from that of a straight dancing club to the topless entertainment. Possibly the ghosts objected. Lights would go on and off at various times—mostly off, as if someone were trying to put a halt to the proceedings.

At first, the manager paid no attention to these reports. Partly he doubted that anything unusual was going on and partly because he felt that such strange phenomena, if they were genuine, could only enhance the attraction of the place for tourists.

But soon he had to revise that view. The tourists who were told that the place might be haunted laughed. They had come to see bodies, not spirits. It was all the same to them. But the girls who worked for the club were another matter. Many came from outlying provinces, little villages, and the backwoods. Their fears were very real. All of a sudden Kerr noticed that his girls would not stay alone in a certain part of the house, especially upstairs. The turnover of personnel at the Mynah was always considerable and did not worry Kerr. To the contrary, he liked to replace his girls frequently since his customers liked to see new faces—or bodies, for that matter. But he began to realize that some of his new girls quit awfully fast. There was no reason for that, since they were always treated decently, customers never got out of line with them, and Mr. Kerr watched over the shows with a sense of pride rather unusual for the operator of a nightclub. Nevertheless, the turnover continued.

Kerr began to question his girls in a calm, low-key voice concerning unusual phenomena they might have observed. At first, the girls did not like to talk, perhaps out of fear of losing their jobs. On the other hand, the uncanny presences in the club also worried them. Before long, the strange occurrences began to happen with greater frequency and seemed to be more definite in character, as if someone or something wanted to make their

presence known in a forceful manner. Musical instruments would move from their proper place by themselves. A male presence spoke to Mr. Kerr's father-in-law upstairs, in the area where the "adult movies" were being shown at the time. Chairs were thrown all over the place in the upstairs room when there had been no one about. Kerr discovered that the theatre where the "adult movies" were being shown was originally an artist's studio. One of the girl dancers felt a man standing close to her, whom she could not see—yet she knew he was angry, and she tried to appease the unseen stranger. Another girl working at the club, also psychic, described the entity as an old man with gray hair and a beard. But there may also be a woman ghost on the premises, judging from the smell of perfume that has been observed at times.

The Mynah Bird is open seven evenings a week, and can be visited freely. In addition to the ghostly performances—which cannot be guaranteed—there are the flesh and blood ones you can always count on and they are sufficient reason to visit.

WEST INDIES

ROSE HALL,
JAMAICA

Sometimes referred to as the most haunted house in the Western Hemisphere, Rose Hall is the great house of Rose Hall Plantation, one of the largest estates of Colonial Jamaica. It has recently been purchased by an American hotelman and meticulously restored to its former glory to be used as a hotel for affluent tourists.

The plantation is not far from the Montego Bay airport, and a good road leads up to it. To this day, some natives will not go near the house, however, referring to it as filled with "goopies," a local term for ghosts. They are indeed right. The earthbound spirit of Annie Porter, once mistress of Rose Hall, has never been laid to rest.

I have been to Rose Hall on two occasions, but without a proper trance medium. It is particularly in the corridors beneath the house that stark terror dwells, and I caution anyone visiting Rose Hall to beware of these areas, especially at night.

Annie Porter was a sadistic woman, who first made lovers of some of her more handsome slaves, and then tortured them to death. Eventually fate caught up with her, and she too was put to death by one of those she had first tormented. Much violence and hatred cling to the old masonry, and is

not likely to have disappeared just because the building had some of its holes filled in and painted over.

The house has three stories and a magnificent staircase out front, by which one gains access to the main floor. It is surrounded by trees and some of the most beautiful landscape in Jamaica. Prior to its restoration, it looked the way a haunted house is always described in fiction or film, with empty windows and broken walls. Now, however, it presents a clean and majestic appearance.

Annie Porter is also referred to as "the White Witch of Rose Hall." There are actually two Annie Porters recorded in history and buried in a nearby cemetery. In the popular legend, the two figures have become amalgamated, but it is the Annie Porter of the late British Colonial period who has committed the atrocities which force her to remain tied to what was once her mansion. I do not doubt that she is still there.

I base this assumption on solid evidence. About ten years ago the late great medium Eileen Garrett paid Rose Hall a visit in the company of distinguished researchers. Her mission was to seek out and, if possible, appease the restless spirit of Annie Porter. Within a matter of moments after her arrival at the Hall, Mrs. Garrett went into a deep trance. The personality of the terror-stricken ghost took over her body, vocal chords, facial expression, and all, and tried to express the pent-up emotions that had so long been dormant.

The researchers were hard pressed to follow the entranced Mrs. Garrett from the terrace, where their quest had begun, through half-dilapidated corridors, underground passages, and dangerously undermined rooms. But Annie Porter wanted them to see the places where she had been the Mistress of Rose Hall, reliving through the medium some of her moments of glory.

Eventually these revived memories led to the point where Annie met her doom at the hand of a young slave with whom she had earlier had an affair.

Crying uncontrollably, writhing on all fours, the medium was by now completely under the control of the restless ghost. No matter how soothingly the researchers spoke to her, asking Annie to let go of the dreadful past, the violent behavior continued. Annie would not leave. In one of the few rare cases on record where a ghost is so tormented and tied to the place of its tragedy that it cannot break away, Annie refused to leave. Instead, the research team left, with a very shaken medium in tow.

ENGLAND

THE GARRICK'S HEAD INN, BATH

Three hours by car from London is the elegant resort city of Bath. Here, in a Regency architectural wonderland, there is an eighteenth-century inn called Garrick's Head Inn. At one time there was a connection between the inn and the theatre next door, but the theatre no longer exists. In the eighteenth century, the famous gambler Beau Nash owned this inn which was then a gambling casino as well.

The downstairs bar looks like any other bar, divided as it is between a large, rather dark room where the customers sip their drinks, and a heavy wooden bar behind which the owner dispenses liquor and small talk. There is an upstairs, however, with a window that, tradition says, is impossible to keep closed for some reason. The rooms upstairs are no longer used for guests, but are mainly storage rooms or private rooms of the owners. At the time of my first visit to the Garricks Head Inn it was owned by Bill Loud, who was a firm skeptic when he had arrived in Bath. Within two months, however, his skepticism was shattered by the phenomena he was able to witness. The heavy till once took off by itself and smashed a chair. The noises of people walking was heard at night at a time when the place was entirely empty. He once walked into what he described as "cobwebs"

and felt his head stroked by a gentle hand. He also smelled perfume when he was entirely alone in the cellar.

A reporter from a Bristol newspaper, who spent the night at the inn, also vouched for the authenticity of the footsteps and strange noises.

Finally the owner decided to dig into the past of the building, and he discovered that there have been incidents which could very well be the basis for the haunting. During the ownership of gambling king Beau Nash, there had been an argument one night, and two men had words over a woman. A duel followed. The winner was to take possession of the girl. One man was killed and the survivor rushed up the stairs to claim his prize. The girl, who had started to flee when she saw him win, was not agreeable, and when she heard him coming barricaded herself in the upstairs room and hanged herself.

Whether you will see or hear the lady ghost at the Garrick's Head Inn in Bath is a matter of individual ability to communicate with the psychic world. It also depends upon the hours of the night you go there, for the Garrick's Head Inn is pretty noisy in the early part of the evening when it is filled with people looking for spirits in the bottle rather than the more ethereal kind.

THE MONKS OF BEAULIEU

Not far from Southampton stands the Abbey of Beaulieu, dating back to the early Middle Ages. It is now mostly a ruin although some parts of it have been restored, especially the Early English refectory or dining hall of the monks, which has been turned into a chapel.

Actually, Beaulieu has two major tourist attractions. One is the old Abbey, the other is Palace House, the residence of the Barons Montagu of Beaulieu, built mainly during the fifteenth century and restored later.

Next to the Palace House, the present Lord Montagu has turned his interest in unusual automobiles into a profitable sideline: the Beaulieu Motor Museum is known the world over. Neither Palace House nor museum has any psychic connotations, of course.

As with many British abbeys or monasteries, the dissolution order of Henry VIII was by no means the end of the presence of monks. Sometimes these people had no other place to go, even in death, and their spirits seem to want to hang on to the old masonry with which they were familiar during their lives.

Ghostly monks have been observed by visitors in the ruined abbey itself and along the pathways leading toward it. In the Beaulieu chapel, once the monks' refectory, two lady visitors saw the scene as it was when the monks used it to dine. Others have heard the choir sing in the empty church. Monks reading scrolls on the stones, walking in what was once a garden, digging a grave in the dead of night to bury one of their own—these are

some of the things that people have reported during the past few years. It is a fact that the monks' own burial ground has never been discovered. There is a cemetery for the villagers, but none of the monks are buried there. Could it be that the restless monks are looking for their own burial ground?

To a visitor, Beaulieu offers many attractions, not the least of which is the possibility of running into a man in a brown habit. If he looks like a monk, please remember—there haven't been any monks at Beaulieu for centuries.

To reach Beaulieu by car from London or from Southampton is quite easy. From London, one has to figure an entire day, getting back late at night. En route, one might conceivably stop at Stonehenge, but there are two or three other attractions of psychic interest in the area that one might go to the following day.

No special permission is required to visit the ruined abbey, but there is a fee for visiting Palace House and it is wise to inquire beforehand if someone might be available to guide you into the haunted portions of the Abbey ruins. One addresses himself to Lord Montagu's factor, or manager, at Palace House, Beaulieu, Hampshire, England.

BISHAM ABBEY

On the Thames River, not far from Marlow, stands one of the finest Tudor buildings in England, called Bisham Abbey. Serving as a priory in the fifteenth century, it became a private house in the sixteenth century and passed into the family of Sir Thomas Hoby. It can easily be reached from London by car or train in somewhat more than an hour. Since it is now a national recreation center for physical recreation activities, and thus a government building, I suppose one can go there without prior appointment. However, getting a guided tour around it is another matter, and I would suggest that any would-be visitor telephone ahead. The warden of the place, when I visited it, was a Mr. Taylor, and either he or his successor no doubt will listen to any reasonable request for a visit.

Built in the traditional Tudor style, the gray walls of the abbey greet one rather magnificently from the driveway. Giving the impression of a palace rather than a church, it has large reception rooms, a magnificent hall, and innumerable bedrooms and other secondary appointments. But it is not the magnificence of the place itself that should be of interest to those reading these lines. One particular room—which was occupied at the time of my visit by the bursar of the establishment, a Mrs. Cecily de Havas—has been the center of ghostly activities for a long time. Knockings from behind the

wall without rational explanation, footsteps, doors seemingly opening of their own volition, and unexplained noises have been observed by a number of people in the building. It doesn't upset them in the least, perhaps because they are aware of the tradition which makes the haunting perfectly expected and, in a way, normal.

Sir Thomas's wife, Elizabeth, had gone to London on one occasion, forgetting completely that she had shut up their child in punishment. She was gone several days, and when she returned the child had died. Unfortunately the harsh treatment given her by her husband did not help her forget her error. To her last days she reproached herself for the death of her child. Since her death, her figure has been observed on a number of occasions, coming from behind the wall in the aforementioned room, with a basin floating ahead of her in which she keeps washing her hands. This apparently is a gesture of cleansing her hands from the blood of her child.

The present inhabitants of the recreation center do not like to discuss this matter, but the legend persists that Elizabeth Hoby is still roaming her onetime domain.

A few years ago, a local historian decided to check whether Mrs. Hoby's child existed, or whether the legend was just that. To his surprise he did find an entry indicating the burial of a small child in the Hoby family, at the period under scrutiny. What made the case even more interesting was a fairly recent report concerning a casual visitor to the grounds. This lady had no knowledge of the legend of Bisham Abbey. On leaving she inquired of the lodgekeeper who the strange-looking, pale woman was she had seen on the lawn. What had particularly puzzled her was the fact the woman wore Elizabethan dress. The lady assumed that a play had been in rehearsal.

Needless to say, there was no play, and the "actress" was probably none other than Lady Hoby projecting her astral self.

I would not advise visitors to stress the psychic aspects of the place when requesting permission to see Bisham. It is a historical building of note, and no such "excuse" is necessary. Many visitors come here without wondering about the ghost.

THE GARGOYLE CLUB, LONDON

Anyone familiar with the London nightclub scene has at one time or another been past a rather garish sign advertising the Gargoyle Club. Together with the Nell Gwyn Theatre, this establishment is housed in what at first appears to be a house of nondescript appearance, but on close examination it clearly shows its age. As a matter of fact, the building itself was erected in 1632 as part of the royal saddlery. Located near the Deanery of St. Paul's, it is now at number 69 Dean Street, and is the property of Jimmie Jacobs, well-known London nightclub entrepreneur. Mr. Jacobs also has the distinction of being a medium and an active member of the spiritualist society of his city.

One gains entrance to the building from a side street, not from Dean Street itself. An elevator goes up to the third floor. It is a very small and slow elevator, in keeping with the narrowness of the stairwell. In addition to the two theatres, one atop the other, there are dressing rooms, an office, and sundry rooms. Finally, there is an open roof on which one can walk up and down.

The insides are no more tawdry than the interior of other nightclubs of this kind. Jimmie Jacobs runs a pretty orderly place, and though his performers do not wear any clothes—or almost none—it is by no means a wide open house in any sense of the term. Prices are modest by American standards, and the shows are not without merit. Various dancers and strippers have at times heard voices, footsteps, seen doors open by themselves, or been disturbed by the noise of documents being handled in total darkness. Some of them had their names called by unseen presences. Mr. Jacobs himself has actually seen a "gray lady" emerge from the elevator shaft, even though the elevator had not opened its doors, and glide by him only to disappear into the opposite wall.

At one time the ancient Royalty Theatre stood next door to the Gargoyle Club, and Jacobs thought for a long time that the ghost was one of the actresses from the Royalty, next door. During the London blitz, the Royalty Theatre was demolished. The phenomenon however continued.

On two separate occasions I took two celebrated London trance mediums to the Gargoyle. They were Ronald Hearn and Miss Trixie Allingham. Independently, however, they insisted that the unrestful presence was Nell Gwyn, and in both cases Nell herself came through in full trance to speak to me of her troubles.

It appears that 69 Dean Street had been Nell Gwyn's private apartment, given to her by King Charles II so that he could have her close by rather than riding off to Salisbury Hall, the country place he had purchased for his beloved Nell. Here, close by Whitehall, the Royal Palace, he could visit her more frequently and with less likelihood of being observed. Unfortunately there were times when Nell was all by herself. It did not suit her theatrical temperament to be neglected, even by so illustrious a suitor as the king. Somehow she struck up an affair with one of the king's officers by the name of Captain John Molyneaux, of the Royal Cavalry. However the king found out. He sent another one of his officers, a Lieutenant Fortescue, with a group of men to the apartment looking for the captain. At the time of the raid, Nell was in the "salon," and Fortescue engaged the captain in a duel on the stairwell. They fought to the finish up the stairs and onto the roof, where Nell's lover fell mortally wounded.

That in essence was the story obtained by psychic means through the mouths of two entranced mediums.

Nell herself was bound to the place not because of King Charles, but because of the death of her lover on the stairs. Whether she herself is still present, or perhaps only the *impression* of her, is hard to say. At any rate, I was able to trace both officers' names in contemporary records, and there is no doubt that number 69 Dean Street was the place of this ancient tragedy.

Mr. Jacobs is also a practical man. His business is to present floor shows and, after the theatrical spectaculars end, more intimate entertainment in a smaller place called the Gargoyle. The personnel doubles from one to the other, and activities at 69 Dean Street last until about three o'clock in the morning. During the day the place is shut down except for an occasional rehearsal in the afternoon. Those who wish to visit the place should call up beforehand since it is nominally at least a club and membership is required. But if Mr. Jacobs is informed of a visitor's interest in the occult, and if he is so inclined, he may very well take such a visitor on a tour after the performance. He might show him the stairwell where some of the members of his troupe have heard uncanny voices, or he might even walk all the way up to the roof and show the door that opens itself at times and some of the haunted dressing rooms.

THE GHOSTLY ANCESTORS AT LONGLEAT

Across England, in the west, and not far from the city of Bath, stands the huge country house Longleat, ancestral seat of the Marquess of Bath. From a distance this white building looks majestic and very much like a fairy tale palace. There are swans in some of the ponds in the large park for which Longleat was famous.

As with so many large estates, the owners had to "go public" to defray the expense of keeping the place in order and pay taxes. Visitors are not only permitted, they are actively encouraged to come. There are extra attractions, such as a zoo with a large number of lions, and dining facilities on the grounds. The ordinary tourist comes for that and the magnificent art in the house. Very few people think of ghosts when visiting Longleat. However, if you wish to see the so-called haunted areas, it would be wiser to write ahead of time and ask for a special tour. Some of these spots are on the "regular" tourist route for all visitors, some are in the private portion of Longleat.

By 1580 the main portion of the house was already in existence, but it was later added to and finally rebuilt in the seventeenth century when it achieved its current appearance. The original owner was a certain Sir John Thynne, a financier to the royal family, who had acquired the property

during a period of stress in English history. He and his successors managed to amass a veritable fortune in fine art and fill Longleat with it from ground floor to the roof. The present Lord Bath lives at a considerably more modest place not far away.

There are three sets of ghosts at Longleat. To begin with, in the so-called red library the apparition of a "scholarly-looking man wearing a high collar and the costume of the sixteenth century" has been seen. He is believed to be the builder of Longleat Sir John Thynne. He may be kept roaming the corridors for personal reasons connected with the acquisition of the property.

Upstairs there is a haunted corridor with a long narrow passage paralleling the bedrooms. It is here that the ghost of Louisa Carteret, one of the ladies in the Bath family, has been repeatedly observed. She has every reason, it appears, to be there. On one occasion she was discovered with a lover by the second Viscount Weymouth, one of Lord Bath's ancestors. A duel was fought by the viscount, and the intruder was killed. Since the viscount had the power of justice in his domain, there was no need for any inquest. The body of the intruder was hurriedly buried in the cellar. A few years ago, when the present Lord Bath was putting in a boiler, the skeleton of the unfortunate lover was accidentally discovered and removed. But Lady Louisa was forever seen looking for her lost lover, and for all I know she may be looking for him still.

Finally, there is a man of the seventeenth century who has been observed in some of the reception rooms downstairs. According to British medium Trixie Allingham, with whom I worked at Longleat, this is the restless ghost of Sir Thomas Thynne, another of Lord Bath's ancestors. Sir Thomas had the misfortune of being betrayed by his wife, it appeared, whose lover had hired two professional assassins to murder the husband. This event took place on the highroad, where the murderers stopped a coach bringing Sir Thomas home, dragged him out and killed him. As sometimes happens with ghosts, he was drawn back to where his emotions were, his home, and apparently he cannot find peace because of the tragic events.

With so many ghosts present at Longleat, the chances of running into one or the other are of course considerably higher than if only an occasional specter were to appear at certain times. But don't expect Longleat ghosts to wait upon you just because you paid your entrance fee or had lunch downstairs in the cafeteria. If you can wrangle a personal introduction to Lord Bath himself, and a private tour into the nontourist areas, then perhaps you might experience some of the things I have been talking about.

SALISBURY HALL, ST. ALBANS

About an hour from London, in the direction of St. Albans, Hertfordshire, stands a moderate-size manor house called Salisbury Hall. The area was settled at a very early period in British history, and within a few miles the Roman city of Verulamium stood, and Roman artifacts are frequently dug out of the soil in and around Salisbury Hall.

Another noteworthy event was the battle of Barnet during which the hall was a fortified strongpoint. Many soldiers died in and around the house, and swords and bones have been found in the moat and garden.

The ground floor of the manor contains several smaller rooms and a very large and impressive room called the crown chamber, with a fireplace on one side. Next to the fireplace there is a door and beyond it a staircase leading to the upper floor.

The area near this staircase is the spot where a number of witnesses have seen the ghost of Nell Gwyn, favorite of Charles II.

It may strike some of my readers as curious that a ghost can appear in more than one location, but Nell Gwyn apparently was partially free and allowed herself to be drawn back to two places connected with her emotional life. Both her city apartment at 69 Dean Street and this country place held deep and precious memories for her, and it is therefore conceivable that she could have been seen at various times in both places. There was no doubt about the identity of the apparition that had been described by Sir Winston Churchill's stepfather, Mr. Cornwallis-West. Less illustrious observers have also seen her.

But in addition to the wraith of Nell, there is also the ghost of a cavaliar who haunts the upstairs part of the hall. At one time there was an additional wing to the building, which no longer exists. It is in the corridor leading to that nonexistent wing that the cavalier has been observed. In one of the rooms at the very end of the corridor, the cavalier is said to have committed suicide when being pursued by soldiers of Oliver Cromwell. He apparently carried some valuable documents on him and did not want to have them fall into the hands of his pursuers; nor did he want to be tortured into telling them anything of value. This was at the height of the Civil War in England, when the Cavaliers—or partisans of the Royalists—were hotly pursued by the parliamentary soldiers, also known as Roundheads. Although the suicide took place in the 1640s, the footsteps of the ghostly Cavalier can still be heard on occasion at Salisbury Hall.

Salisbury Hall belongs to Walter Goldsmith who lives there with his wife and children. He is an artist by profession but has lately turned the hall into a part-time tourist attraction on certain days of the week. Since he has spent great sums of money to restore the manor from the state of disrepair in which he bought it, one can hardly blame him for the modest fee of admission required for a visit. Mr. Goldsmith will gladly point out the haunted spots and discuss psychic phenomena without denying their reality, especially in his house.

HAUNTED SAWSTON HALL, CAMBRIDGESHIRE

A short distance from the great English university town of Cambridge, off the main road, lies Sawston Hall, a Catholic stronghold that has been in the Huddleston family for many generations. It is an imposing, gray stone structure, three stories high and surrounded by a lovely garden. It is so secluded that it is sometimes hard to locate unless one knows exactly where to turn off the main road. Inside, the great hall is a major accomplishment of Tudor architecture, and there are many large rooms, bedrooms, and galleries. Sawston Hall represents the very best in English Tudor architecture. Its size lies somewhere between the great houses of royalty and the baronial estates which dot the English countryside by the hundreds.

Sawston Hall can be visited by the public on certain days and by prearrangement. The man to contact is Major A. C. Eyre, nephew of the late Captain Huddleston, who manages the estate.

The principal personality associated with Sawston Hall is Queen Mary Tudor, sometimes called Bloody Mary. She rebuilt Sawston Hall after her enemies had burned it down. Her favorite room was a drawing room with a virginal, a sixteenth-century musical instrument.

From the drawing room, one goes through a corridor called the Little Gallery, and a paneled bedroom, into the Tapestry Bedroom which is named for a large set of Flemish tapestries on the wall, depicting the life of King

Solomon. In the center of this room is a four poster in which Queen Mary allegedly slept. In the wall behind the bed is a door through which her ghost is said to have appeared on several occasions. Behind that door lies a passage leading to a so-called priest's hole, a secret hiding place where Catholic priests were hidden during the turbulent times of the religious wars in the sixteenth century. Whenever Protestant raiders came, the priests would hide themselves in these prearranged hiding places which were well supplied with air, water, and food. As soon as everything was clear, the priests would reemerge to join the Catholic household.

A number of people who have slept in what is called Queen Mary's room, in the fourposter, have reported uncanny experiences. It is always the same story: three knocks at the door, then the door opens by itself and a gray form slowly floats across the room and disappears into the tapestry. Many have heard the virginal play soft music when there was no one in the drawing room. It is a fact that the young Princess Mary was expert at this instrument, and on numerous occasions was asked to play to show her musical talents.

In 1553, Princess Mary was living in Norfolk, when her half-brother Edward VI died. The Duke of Northumberland, who then dominated the English government, did not want her to succeed to the throne, but wanted instead to have a member of his own family rule England. A false message was sent to Mary purporting to come from her ailing brother Edward. It was in fact a trap set for her by the Duke of Northumberland to lure her to London where he could dispose of her. When Mary reached Sawston Hall on her way to the capital, she received word of the real situation. She immediately fled back to Norfolk. When they discovered that their prey had escaped, the troops of the Duke of Northumberland were enraged and set fire to Sawston Hall. Looking back on the smoldering ruins of Sawston Hall, Mary said to John Huddleston that she would build him a greater hall than ever once she came to the throne. Not much later she kept her word, and Sawston Hall is the building created during the reign of Mary Tudor. It is not surprising that her spirit should be drawn back to a place that actually saved her life at one time, where she found more love than at any other place in England. Mary Tudor was herself a Catholic, as were the Huddlestons, and thus Sawston Hall does represent the kind of emotional tie I have found to be necessary for ghostly manifestation.

Visitors to the hall may not encounter the ghost of Mary Tudor, but then again, one never knows. There are also other presences in this ancient house, but they seem to be concentrated in the upstairs part. The great hall, the little gallery, and Mary's bedroom are all the domain of "the gray lady."

STONEHENGE

Although Stonehenge is not a haunted house, it is well worth a visit for anyone interested in the possibility of picking up vibrations from the past. Stonehenge is an ancient circle of stones aligned in a mathematically correct manner so that they can be used as an observatory to measure time, the movement of the stars, and possibly weather conditions. There are many books dealing with this amazing monument, but the fact is that it was not built by the Druids, as is often said, but taken over by the Druids from its earlier owners. These were the witches of Britain who had built and used Stonehenge as a sanctuary.

About two hours south of London on the direct road to Southampton, Stonehenge lies right off the main road. A small payment is exacted by the overseer of the ruins. As a major British tourist attraction, it is never empty of people, and it might be difficult to find a time of day when one can meditate or rest in the area. Certainly weekends are to be avoided at all costs.

Eileen Garrett, the late medium and psychic researcher, "sat" on Stonehenge's stones and vividly relived ancient sacrificial ceremonies. She saw people in white robes chanting and performing ritual movements. Sybil Leek came to Stonehenge in my company and in a state bordering on trance relived some of the scenes from the past.

Ritual sacrifice of human beings has sometimes been attributed to the ancient Druids, even though their modern successors the Order of Druids do not like to dwell on that aspect of the religion.

The scene felt by both Eileen Garrett and Sybil Leek undoubtedly was an imprint of the Druidic past. A young man was selected to be killed ritually as a token of payment for favors the community wanted to ask the gods. Not the weak or old or prisoners of war were used in such rituals, but on the contrary a youth of great strength and valor was selected to be the victim.

But human sacrifice was not native to Britain before the arrival of the Druids. The Wicca people, better known as the followers of witchcraft or "the old religion," who built Stonehenge, had no use for blood sacrifice. The main theme of their religion was firm belief in reincarnation and to take a man's life would have created negative karma for those who sacrificed him.

The Druids came to Britain by sea, from the Mediterranean lands of pre-Hellenic Greece. It is therefore interesting to note that Sybil Leek had in a semitrance state spoken of Greek men with Greek names who came to worship at Stonehenge.

For any sensitive visitor to come to Stonehenge and not feel some of the highly charged atmospheric vibrations is impossible. A visit can be combined with a trip to Beaulieu or Stonehenge can be seen on the way to Longleat and the west.

SCOTLAND

HERMITAGE CASTLE

The dividing line between Scotland and England is known as border country. It is wild and remote, and the roads are far from good. At night you can very easily get lost there, but it is well worth the drive down from Edinburgh to Hermitage Castle, which is located outside the town of Hawick.

The area has a long history of warfare, even in peacetime. When Scotland and England were not yet joined together as one kingdom, this area was filled with lawlessness, and raids in one or the other direction were common. The lords of the area had a nasty habit of throwing their enemies into dungeons and letting them die of starvation there. One of the more sinister places in the area, Hermitage was built in the early Middle Ages and has long been associated with the Soulis family. It was here that the Earl of Bothwell, who later became her husband, was visited by Mary Queen of Scots, in 1566.

From the outside the castle looks very much the way it did when it was built in the thirteenth century. It consists of two main towers built of rough stones connected in such a manner that the fortress could withstand almost any attack. The entrance gate was well above ground, to prevent enemies from crashing it. Inside, most of the subdivisions no longer exist;

but enough of the castle has been restored so that one can walk about and view what was once a reasonably comfortable dwelling—by early medieval standards.

In those far-off days, nobody trusted his neighbors. Petty wars and family feuds were the rule among the nobles of Scotland. When a neighboring chief sent a group of goodwill ambassadors to Hermitage to propose cessation of their long feud, the lord of the manor promptly put the men into a small room without food or water. They died there miserably and their ghosts are said to be among the many who still stalk the ruins.

On another occasion, the ruling Lord Soulis invited a number of local chiefs and nobles to a banquet in honor of the marriage of one of his daughters. Access to the castle was one flight up, not on the ground level. This was a defense measure, so that the castle could be defended by simply pulling up the wooden stairs leading from the ground to the first floor. As soon as the guests had all arrived and were seated in the banquet hall upstairs, the ladder was withdrawn and the gate closed by previous arrangement. The plan was to feed the guests first and murder them afterward.

However, the ladder need not have been withdrawn. As an afterthought Lord Soulis had instructed his cook to put poison into the food of his guests

and it worked so well they were all dead before the last course of the banquet.

Individual enemies were not fed first and killed later: they were simply taken below, to the dungeon at the cellar level, which had and still has a clammy, cold stone floor made of roughly cut rocks. The most frightening spot in the building is a small hole in the stone floor. Enemies were pushed through this hole into the dungeon below, never to see the light of day again. Even their remains were not removed.

I do not doubt that Hermitage is still covered with impressions from its cruel past. Not only are the unhappy spirits of the victims felt in the atmosphere by anyone sensitive enough to do so, but there is still another reason why Hermitage is considered different from ordinary castles. One of the owners, Lord Soulis, was a black magician and had committed a number of documented atrocities. Finally the people of the countryside got together and seized him. Taking their inspiration from Lord Soulis' own way of life, they dispatched him in a most frightful manner by tying him with lead bands and then boiling him over a fire. According to the *Blue Guide to Scotland*: "To the E. [of Hermitage] is *Nine Stane Rig*, a hill with a stone circle, where the cruel Lord Soulis is said to have been boiled alive by his infuriated vassals. In reality Lord Soulis died in prison at Dumbarton

Castle." But according to local talk his ghost is in evidence still at the castle—especially on the anniversary of his death.

Hermitage Castle can be visited without difficulty or previous arrangement. There is a custodian on the premises, who for a small fee readily takes you on a guided tour. The house is now a kind of museum. There are no accommodations for sleeping in it, nor would I advise anyone to try.

IRELAND

THE DANISH SAILOR OF
BALLYHEIGUE

Ballyheigue is not the name of a popular song by Rodgers and Hammerstein, but a castle standing in one of the most picturesque and at the same time most lonely spots in all Ireland. It stands on a gentle slope looking down into the bay of Kerry in southwestern Ireland, and there is only a very small village by the same name nearby. You must ride for hours to get there from any large cities such as Tralee, and it is even farther from Shannon or Limerick. But it is worth every moment of the long and sometimes uncomfortable drive.

The roads in this part of Ireland are far from perfect, and the final part of the way is almost only a cow path.

Ballyheigue great house was burned down in what the Irish like to refer to as "the Troubles"—that is to say, the insurrection in which many of the English-owned manor houses were burned down in a display of frustration. Today it is nothing but an empty shell of its former self. Its turreted roofs are gone except for the outer walls, and where once the noble gentry of southwestern Ireland dined and danced, there are now just gaping holes.

When you leave the car at the entrance gate to the estate in order to walk the last few yards up the hill to the castle, you must be careful not to slip as the meadow has been used extensively for grazing purposes, and cows dot the landscape. There is no one to prevent you from entering the ruined great house itself. Occasionally there seems to be a sort of gatekeeper, and half a crown is collected from curious visitors. No one takes you around the ruined house. You proceed at your own risk. This risk may include running into the ghost of a Danish sailor who has not been dislodged either by time nor by my expedition there some years back in the company of Sybil Leek. All she could do was make contact with him in a vague and sort of indirect way. Perhaps the moment was not right or perhaps his continued presence was still required to guard the treasure. And thereby hangs the ghostly tale of Ballyheigue Castle.

The area was and perhaps still is a haven for smugglers. Today smuggling is carried on in a refined and minor manner if at all. But in the eighteenth century it was a major profession and many of the landed gentry who had houses along the coast were either actively or secretly involved in these enterprises. Most of the smuggling was done by ship from the continent or from England and involved fine yard goods, silver and gold, liquor, and other goods of sophistication that were scarce in rural Ireland.

Ballyheigue was already old in 1730 when the old Kerry records show that a Danish ship called *The Golden Lyon* was passing by this part of the coast on her way from the Indies to Denmark. She was blown off course by a storm and could be plainly seen from the land. The Crosbies, owners of Ballyheigue Castle at that time, set up false lights on horses' heads to lure the ship even closer to shore, and sure enough, she was wrecked on the rocky Kerry coast. Thereupon Sir Thomas Crosbie sent out a crew to rescue the sailors of the Danish ship and to salvage what was left of her cargo. Among the latter were twelve cases of silver bars and coin. The cargo was safely stored in the vaults of Ballyheigue Castle, and the survivors were treated as honored guests by the owners of the castle.

But the precious secret of the vault took its toll. First it was Sir Thomas himself who died suddenly, it was rumored by poison. The captain of the ship tried to get his cargo out of the castle walls, but the crafty widow of Sir Thomas had tied up the rights to it in a trumped-up suit for salvage and the loss of her husband.

A year later the captain was still unable to leave Ballyheigue Castle and so was the silver. One night the good captain was awakened by the sound of voices and realized that fifty or sixty men with blackened faces were storming the gates of the castle. Lady Margaret, the widow, begged the captain not to oppose the raiders or he might be killed. The raiders took away the silver chests and left many of the Danes dead on the spot.

Unfortunately, one of the Danes had seen Lady Margaret's nephew among the intruders, so it became clear that the raid had been undertaken with the knowledge and participation of the owner of the castle. Most of the raiders were later caught and some were executed, but the silver was never completely recovered, and no one knows where three-quarters of it went. Some say it was buried somewhere nearby.

In 1962, a certain Captain P. D. O'Donnell arrived at Ballyheigue on a vacation. On the very anniversary of the Danish silver raid, he took some snapshots in the ruined castle. Imagine his surprise when one of the pictures showed—in addition to the captain's nephew Frank—the figure of a Danish swordsman standing near a window. The figure wore high boots and clothes of the eighteenth century. On examination, the Captain realized that he had chanced into Ballyheigue Castle on the very anniversary of the event. The Captain later lost this snapshot.

Sybil Leek picked up much of the original story in bits and pieces. She felt the underground passage connecting the castle with the sea, and delineated the influence of a woman with the event in question. She felt that a man had been poisoned, and at once I thought of Sir Thomas and Lady Margaret.

The ghosts at Ballyheigue include the Danish sailor standing guard over the silver and fencing off the Irish raiders; and perhaps also Lady Margaret, whose guilt may very well still tie her to what was once her home.

Those coming to Ballyheigue the night of June 4 are well advised to bring a camera, just in case one or the other ghost may pose for a picture.

THE LOVERS OF CARLINGFORD

Carlingford Castle and Abbey—or what's left of them, which isn't very much except ruins—stand near the shore of Lough Carlingford in northeastern Ireland, facing England across the sea in one direction, and Northern Ireland in the other. The sea can be quite rough at times in this bay, and there is a certain romantic wildness to the scenery even in the summer. Walking amidst the ruins of what was once an imposing castle and abbey, one gets the feeling of time standing still and also sometimes of an eerie presence. James Reynolds in *More Ghosts in Irish Houses*, reports how an English traveler, who was totally unaware of the haunting reported in these ruins, saw a shadowy figure of a woman and of a man standing in what was once a chapel, only to merge and disappear into the night.

When I visited the ruins of Carlingford with Sybil Leek, she too felt the presence of something unearthly—but to her these ghosts were not frightening or unhappy. Rather she felt a kind of love imprint from the past, something that came and went but somehow was tied to these rocks.

There is a small piece of land between the ruins and the sea, and a road leading down toward it. From the ruined wall of Carlingford all the way down to the shore seems to be the haunted area, or at any rate the area most likely to give a sensitive person the feeling of a presence.

What is left of Carlingford Castle and Abbey is nothing more than a few stone walls without roofs, and a few impressive arches and glassless windows. What was once the chapel, however, is fairly well preserved even though it has neither roof nor floor, nor in fact anything whatsoever to worship by. The niche above the altar is now empty, but it contained a statue of the Virgin at one time.

Who then are the ghostly figures seen by the English tourist? In the first part of the fifteenth century a lady pirate by the name of Henrietta Travescant, after giving up the sea, retired to Carlingford Abbey to serve as its head. Her ship in her active pirate days had been called *The Black Abbess*, so she took the same name when she became the resident abbess of Carlingford.

Perhaps what had prompted her to give up her cherished sea was not only her patriotic desire to give her ship to King Henry V, whom she supported, to serve in his war against France, but also her unhappiness at the loss of her beloved Nevin O'Neill, whom the cruel sea had taken during one of their expeditions.

According to the legend as told by James Reynolds, the years passed by and soon the Black Abbess found herself practically alone in the rambling and partially dilapidated castle and abbey at Carlingford. One night when praying in front of the madonna, she heard the voice of her dead lover calling to her from out of the mist. Not sure of his identity, she is said to have demanded proof that it was really he who was calling out to her. Soon after, she heard him again calling her from the seashore, ran down toward the sea, and was swallowed up by a huge breaker, never to be found again.

It is her ghost, and that of Nevin O'Neill, who have often been seen walking by the rocky seashore or standing together in the ruined chapel. Quiet summer nights, close to midnight, are the best time to run into this phenomenon—if you are one of those who are capable of registering the very tenuous vibrations of such a haunting.

Carlingford is now only a small town, but at one time in the seventeenth century it was large enough to be the temporary capital of Ireland, and a parliament was once in session there. One reaches Carlingford either by railroad to Dundalk and then about eight miles by car over a winding but otherwise good road, or one can go all the way from Dublin by car. Carlingford is equidistant from Dublin and Belfast. The ruins can be reached on foot only, directly from the village. Like so many other Irish towns, its population has dwindled over the years, and it is now actually more like a village than a small town. But the people of Carlingford are still proud of it and prefer to call it a town.

A DONNYBROOK MANSION, DUBLIN

When most people hear the word donnybrook, they think of a fistfight among Irishmen, but the fact is that Donnybrook is a well-to-do suburb of Dublin. The word Donnybrook itself is derived from St. Broc, a local saint. There is a secret well on the grounds of the very house we are about to discuss. It is dedicated to this saint. It may well be that the entire area took its name from this spot.

The house is called Ballinguile, and I wrote of it for the first time in *The Lively Ghosts of Ireland*. The house is located at 8, Eglington Road. Set back somewhat from the tree-lined avenue, it has an aristocratic exterior even though at the time I first saw it, in 1965, it was already beginning to fall into decay. When I visited it again in 1969, the destruction had gone even further. Partially due to lack of care, the weather—which in Ireland is wet and frequently cold—and partially due to teen-age gangs who threw stones through its windows, the house had taken on the look of neglect.

It is rather large and must have been a country house at one time, because it is still surrounded by a lush green lawn and what must once have been a very well-tended vegetable garden. Today it is all wilderness. Farther back there is what used to be a small compact gatehouse, which had for years been rented to a separate tenant, who was also supposed to look after the main house.

The last time I saw the house, the tenant had gone too, and the only way you could get access was by calling the owner, Arthur Lurie, a Dublin real estate man. I doubt, however, that a request to visit Ballinguile because it was haunted would get much sympathy from Mr. Lurie, who is a very practical man of central European background. If, on the other had, one were to inquire on the grounds that one had an interest in purchasing the property, especially to build a new house on the lot, Mr. Lurie might conceivably be more interested. Those among my readers who are wealthy enough to buy their own haunted house should be warned, however, that the property is now worth somewhere around $100,000 because it is located in one of the best sections of Dublin, and it is large enough to build a modern apartment house on.

If you are fortunate enough—or perhaps adventurous enough—to enter the house itself, past the boarded-up doors and broken windows, you will find it rather comfortable in the sense that the rooms are all very large, both the sitting rooms downstairs and the bedrooms upstairs. The house, however, is built in a very haphazard fashion, and has been added to from time to time.

Above the second story containing the bedrooms there is an attic, to which one can gain access only by a metal ladder. On one side of the building is an old greenhouse now fallen into decay, and farther back there are stables for horses and other animals.

Although the plot of land is not terribly large, the position of the house is such that it gives the impression of being secluded and private, and it seems more like a country estate than a city house.

The house was first brought to my attention by Mrs. Mary Healy who had lived in it for many years. What convinced Mrs. Healy that her house was haunted were the sounds of footsteps, mostly on the stairs, which seemed to her so natural that she did not immediately realize they were not made by any flesh and blood human being. Most of these footsteps occurred during the daytime, and in particular during the summer months.

One night in August, Mrs. Healy's son went out in the evening for a while, leaving Mrs. Healy alone in the house. Shortly after she had gone to bed, she awoke to hear a lot of people downstairs, laughing, talking, and moving around. Immediately she thought that her son had brought his friends back to the house and that the boys were having a party downstairs. She wished that he had told her of his intentions, and promised herself to question him about it in the morning. A short time later, her son returned. She immediately asked him about the noise. There had been no party downstairs.

But her son was not the only one who experienced strange things at the house. Her little girl kept talking about a "tall, dark man" she had seen in the yard. No one else had seen this man.

The local police began to wonder about Ballinguile. Grapevine had it that the owners were frequently quarreling. On one occasion two passing policemen clearly heard the noise of a violent argument from inside the house. The voices were so loud they decided to investigate and rang the doorbell. The owners were quite surprised by their visit. So were the two policemen, since the voices had stopped abruptly the moment the door was opened.

Sybil Leek came with me to Ballinguile without knowing anything about the house or its former occupants. But the moment she set foot into the garden, she felt a psychic presence. She pointed to one of the upper rooms and explained that she felt a man up there. We entered and I followed her up the rickety stairs. When we arrived in the corner room upstairs, Sybil was almost in trance. She was able to describe a man looking a little like Abraham Lincoln, as she put it. About fifty years ago this man had been involved in a plot of sorts concerning some papers which were not what they were supposed to have been. She also managed to get a name sounding like Whibern, and intimated that he could not find rest until the deeds were put in order. Someone named Miss Seamly had made a mistake, the medium explained, and the ground had not been measured correctly in the records. I knew, of course, that the house was three hundred years old, and I asked Mrs. Leek to pinpoint a date, if possible, for the story she was telling me. The best she could do was mention the year 1924.

When Mrs. Leek was in full trance, the entity himself spoke to me, thanking me for having come to the house and asking that we help him straighten the records. He wanted the land to go to an institute for sick people. The name that had come to her all along was either Whibern or perhaps White. In fact, Mrs. Leek had spoken about a man named White ever since we had met up in Dublin prior to coming to this house.

On checking the background of the house I discovered that a Mr. Bantry White used to live in the house. There had been some difficulty about the land ownership. Sybil had been right about that. However, it was much too late to do anything about it.

On my first visit to Ballinguile I had stepped into the downstairs parlor all by myself, leaving my wife and Sybil somewhat behind. It was then that I clearly heard human voices speaking in subdued tones. At the time I was surprised and I immediately assumed that the real estate people had sent someone else to look at the house while we were there. I looked around the house very carefully. I was quite alone; and yet I am sure I heard those voices too! So if you manage to get permission to visit Ballinguile, walk around quietly and listen, and perhaps you too might hear the voices.

KILKEA CASTLE, KILDARE

From a distance, Kilkea Castle looks the very image of an Irish castle. Turreted, gray, proud, sticking up from the landscape with narrow and tall windows which give it a massive and fortified appearance, Kilkea Castle is nevertheless one of the most comfortable tourist hotels in present-day Ireland. Anyone may go there simply by making a reservation with the genial host, Dr. William Cade.

The castle is about an hour and a half by car from Dublin, in the middle of fertile farmlands. There are beautiful walks all around it, and the grounds are filled with brooks, old trees, and meadows—the latter populated by a fairly large number of cows.

Kilkea was built in 1180 by an Anglo-Norman knight named Sir Walter de Riddleford, and it is said to be the oldest inhabited castle in Ireland, although I have seen this claim put forward in regard to several places. Let there be no mistake: the inside has been modified and very little of the original castle remains. But the haunting is still there.

The castle has four floors, not counting cellars and roof. The rooms are of varying sizes and kinds. The haunted area is actually what must have been the servants' quarters at one time, and it is reached through a narrow passage in the northern section of the castle. The room itself is just large enough for one person, and if you should want to sleep in it, you had better make a reservation way ahead of time. All you need to do is ask Dr. Cade for the haunted room. He will understand.

The story of the haunting goes back to the early Middle Ages. Apparently one of the beautiful daughters of an early owner fell in love with a stableboy. Her proud father disapproved and threatened to kill them both if they continued their association. One night, the father found the young man in his daughter's room. In the struggle that followed the boy was killed, but we are not told whether the girl was killed or not. But it is the boy's ghost who apparently still roams the corridors, trying to get his sweetheart back.

In the course of rebuilding, this room became part of the servants' quarters. A number of people have reported uncanny feelings in the area. The owner of Kilkea himself, though skeptical, has admitted to witnessing doors opening by themselves for no apparent reason.

Locally, the so-called Wizard Earl is blamed for the happenings at Kilkea Castle, and there is even a legend about him. Apparently to please his lady fair, the earl transformed himself into a bird and sat on her shoulder. But he had not counted on the presence of the castle cat, who jumped up and ate the bird. The legend continues that the earl and his companions still ride at night and will eventually return from the beyond to "put things right in Ireland"—if that is necessary. The legend does not say what happened to the cat.

RENVYLE, CONNEMARA

Today Renvyle House is a first-rate hotel looking out onto the western-most tip of Ireland. It is the nearest point to the United States. It is cold and windy at times, but during the summer months can be pleasant and warm. The accommodations are first class even though limited, because Renvyle House is not very large as hotels go.

Most of the tourists who come to Renvyle are from England, with an occasional sprinkling of Americans. Originally the house was owned by the family of St. John Gogarty, the famous literary figure. The house stood on the site of the original Gogarty House, which burned down during the so-called "Troubles." Although the present structure was built in 1932, it seems to have inherited some of the hauntings of the past.

As soon as the house had been rebuilt, Mr. Gogarty ran it as a kind of hotel for literary figures of his day. W. B. Yeats made it almost a second home. Many séances were held there, and on one such occasion something was dredged up from the past of Renvyle House that wouldn't go away.

Built like a western Irish country manor, the house is white and brown, the bottom part consisting of stone and the top portion of wood. The shingled roof is of a grayish color. To reach it, one must go to Galway and it takes as much as three hours to Renvyle by car since the roads are far from good. But the trip is definitely worthwhile.

Prior to the acquisition of the place by St. John Gogarty, the house had been the seat of the Blake family. The haunted rooms seem to be number 27, number 2, and possibly number 38. It all started after a séance held during the St. John Gogarty ownership of the place, when one of the Blake children evidently materialized before the astonished assembly.

St. John Gogarty himself reported this incident in an article in *Tomorrow* magazine in 1952. Eoin Dillon, a former manager of Renvyle House, reported that on several occasions people complained that a stranger was in their rooms. What was more, the stranger disappeared rather suddenly, without benefit of door. Mr. Dillon himself heard finger-clicking noises when he slept in the room once used by Yeats for the séances. He decided to pull the blanket over his ears and let the matter clear itself up. A maid also had seen a man in one of the upstairs corridors disappear before her eyes into thin air. When she described the stranger, it developed that he looked a great deal like the late W. B. Yeats. The apparition was seen about lunchtime in 1966, and one must remember that Yeats did indeed consider Renvyle House a second home. It is entirely conceivable that someone coming to Renvyle House in the future, possessed of the right psychic abilities, might encounter one of those staying behind, beyond flesh and blood—either the Blake boy or perhaps the great poet himself.

Ross House
Mayo.
Ireland

C. Budreanton
8-66

ROSS HOUSE,
COUNTY MAYO

Ross House is not open to the public. I am stating this clearly so that those who wish to visit it should not be disappointed if their request for admission is ignored or denied. Major M. J. Blackwell, part of the famous firm of Crosse & Blackwell, is a prominent citizen of Chicago, Illinois, and is bound to have many friends—and his friends no doubt have friends, so that it is not entirely inconceivable that a letter requesting permission to visit Ross House might just be answered in the affirmative. Under no circumstances do I advise anyone to arrive at Ross House unexpectedly and unannounced. This applies as much to Ross House as to any other haunted private dwelling. Even in Ireland, where there are fewer telephones than elsewhere, and where friends are in the habit of dropping in on each other, it is not advisable for a stranger to be that presumptuous. But Ross House represents such a picturesque and unusual aspect of haunting that I felt I must include it here.

The house itself is located in a perfect spot, looking out over Clew Bay, halfway between Westport and Newport in County Mayo. From the windows you can look out on the many islands that dot the bay, two of which also belong to the owners of Ross House. This is a major estate, left largely untouched by the vicissitudes of time and financial changes. The house is

Georgian and is furnished in the style of the period. There are large reception rooms downstairs on both sides of a magnificent Georgian staircase, and bedrooms upstairs, all looking out onto the bay. Major Blackwell inherited the house from his mother, who was a descendant of the famous O'Malley clan. Perhaps the best known of the O'Malleys was Grania O'Malley, the pirate queen of the sixteenth century who considered herself a true equal to Queen Elizabeth of England and was actually received by the Queen at court.

English born, the major, who lives in a Chicago suburb, inherited Ross House in 1960. He had spent many weeks at a time at the house during his childhood and was very familiar with it. The local people considered him one of their own, which is something of an accomplishment since the fishermen of the area are extremely close knit and generally hostile to strangers.

In the back of the house there is a very ancient tomb dating back to the very dawn of Irish history. The tomb is that of Dermott MacGrania, who was killed with his mother, Grania, and buried in it about 1500 B.C. Once when the major, an avid amateur archaeologist, tried to dig up the tomb, he found himself frightened by a vivid vision the following night, in which he saw the apparition of Dermott MacGrania himself threatening him if he continued to disturb his peace and grave. The major has not touched it since.

Another earlier house stood on this spot prior to the Georgian one. Christianity goes back a long time in this area, and there is a ruined monastery on one of the two islands belonging to the estate.

Six years before my visit with the major he had been asleep in one of the rooms upstairs when he awoke to find the old maidservant Annie O'Flynn standing at the end of his bed. With her was another woman. The major could see them both clearly and pointed them out to his wife who, however, could not see anything. The major remembered Annie O'Flynn because she had been his grandmother's maid. The next day he went to talk to Tommie Moran, an old man who worked on the estate, and described the other woman ghost he had seen. Moran immediately identified her as a close friend of the late maid's, who had also died sometime back.

A cousin of the major's, Linda Carvel, had seen the old maidservant walking up and down the staircase, and both the major and his wife had heard footsteps at various times in a spot where the original stairs used to be. Sometimes there is a knock at the bedroom door, as if a maid were ready to serve breakfast. Miss Carvel actually saw Annie O'Flynn dressed in a starched white and blue uniform, such as the maids of the period used to wear. The fact is that the maidservant was closely attached to the family and returned frequently to the house even after she had left and gotten married. There is no doubt that Annie O'Flynn likes to serve the major's family and doesn't take kindly to the idea of being dead. In Ireland, the line between the living and the dead is drawn rather loosely anyway.

MURDER AT SKRYNE CASTLE

James Reynolds first mentioned Skryne Castle in *More Ghosts in Irish Houses*, and I reported my visit there in *The Lively Ghosts of Ireland*. The castle is not far from renowned Tara, ancient capital of Ireland—or what remains of it which is nothing more than a few hills since Tara was built entirely of wood. But it is an easy ride from Dublin and one can combine a visit to Tara with a short stay at Skryne Castle.

Built in 1172, the ancient house fell into disrepair and was not rebuilt until early in the nineteenth century. Today it looks much more like a Victorian country home than an ancient castle. The walls are covered with ivy and the roof is surmounted by a small tower and turret in the fashion of the Victorian Age. This style was popular when builders fancied themselves the romantic successors to the castle builders of the Middle Ages and liked to imitate what they thought was the proper style of the twelfth century, but which in fact is nothing more than a nineteenth-century imitation.

Still, Skryne is an imposing building, especially when one drives up from the village and sees it looming behind the ancient trees on both sides of the driveway. Apparently the present owners use the house for catering now and again, renting it out for wedding parties and such. It is therefore semi-private—or rather, semipublic—and one can make arrangements for a visit by telephoning ahead, although we took a chance and simply drove up, asking for permission to enter when we arrived.

The upstairs salon to the right of the staircase is the one Sybil Leek felt to be the most haunted. There were several layers of ghostly happenings in the atmosphere, she explained—one having to do with a courier arriving at the house half dead and unable to save himself. That one, however, goes back to the Middle Ages. Sybil received the impression that the man spoke of the fianna, a word that meant nothing to me at the time. But I discovered later that the fianna were a group of nobles who had rebelled against the high king Cairbre around A.D. 597, and that a battle had indeed been fought between the rebels and the king at the very foot of Skryne Castle.

The specter in the house, however, was female and according to Mrs. Leek her name was something like *Mathilda*. According to Reynolds, however, the girl's name was *Lilith* Palmerston, and the tragedy that ended her life happened in 1740 when the house was owned by Sir Bromley Casway. Lilith was his beautiful ward, and during her long stay at Skryne Castle the young girl had met a young man named Phelim Sellers who lived not far from Skryne. Unfortunately he fell in love with Lilith, but she was unable to return his feelings. Finally Sir Bromley decided to take his beautiful ward back to Dublin to escape the attentions of the unwanted suitor. The night before their planned departure for Dublin, however, Sellers got wind of their intent, broke into Skryne Castle, entered the girl's room and strangled her. He was hanged for his crime at Galway City.

It is the girl's unhappy presence that has been felt on many occasions by those who have slept in what used to be her room. One man saw what he thought was a nun, who dissolved before his very eyes. A Mrs. Riley who often worked in Skryne Castle had heard footsteps when no one was walking.

If you are in the vicinity, call upon the owner whose name is Nichols. Better yet, drop a line ahead of time. The Irish are very hospitable, but they do like to know whom to expect. Exceptions are made only for ghosts.

GARDENER'S COTTAGE, WICKLOW

At Baltinglass, in County Wicklow, about an hour and a half south of Dublin, lies an estate called Slaney Park. It belongs to the Grogan family and is private property. But the Grogans are intelligent and sociable people and might welcome a visitor, provided he approached them the right way, ahead of time, and with a polite request to have a look at the haunted cottage. I am not guaranteeing this, mind you, but I have a feeling that the Grogans wouldn't mind an occasional visitor from the States.

John Grogan is a gentleman farmer, and the cottage caused him a number of problems—that is, it used to, prior to our visit there in the company of Sybil Leek. The cottage is large enough to be considered a house by American standards. It stands a considerable distance from the main house, at the edge of a field, surrounded by shrubbery. Its two stories and vaulted rooms give it the impression of a small manor house rather than a gardener's cottage. Built of brick and stone and painted white on the outside, it had fallen into disrepair at the time we visited it.

The main house, which is not haunted, was built in the period prior to 1755, when the Grogan family acquired the property from the Crosbys. The cottage, however, had been the center of unusual activity for many years past. No one wanted to stay there very long and the Grogans had great

trouble keeping a gardener in this lodge.

Every Thursday evening the place came alive: there were knockings, teacups disappeared by themselves, and a cold clammy atmosphere made the place very inhospitable. Whether or not there is some unpleasantness hanging on from the earlier period of the cottage is hard to determine. The principal disturbance, however, dates back only about sixty-five years. A Scottish gardener, whom Mrs. Leek had psychically identified as Drummond, had lived there with his wife. Their marriage had not been a happy one. One day, the wife invited her sister to stay with them and share the cottage. Unfortunately, the gardener and the sister became involved with each other. When the wife found out, she forced the sister to leave the house. To make sure that her sister actually left, she took her to the train at Baltinglass station. When she returned to the cottage, she found that the house was locked. Puzzled by this, she went to the main house and asked for help. The great-grandmother of the present owners came back with her to the cottage and together they broke open the door. Silence greeted them. They walked about the house, looking in vain for Mr. Drummond. Walking up the stairs to the bedroom, they found why the house had been so silent. There he was, hanging from the bannister. He had committed suicide upstairs while his wife was away putting her sister on the train. That was on a Thursday night, and ever since then, the knocking and strange goings-on have recurred at the identical time and day the gardener died.

Baltinglass can be reached by either train or bus, but the best way is by private car. There is a fairly good inn in the village, and if you are fortunate enough to be permitted access to the cottage by John Grogan, it would be better to go down to Baltinglass in the morning, have lunch in the village, and go to the estate right after lunch as we did. The landscape is beautiful, and the cottage itself is surrounded by tall trees and rolling meadows. Don't look for the ghost of the gardener, however, because I am pretty sure Mrs. Leek was able to pry him loose from the scene of his great tragedy. If you happen to be psychic perhaps you will relive the entire tragedy, since the impression is still in the atmosphere even though the principals may have left.

WEST TOWN HOUSE, NAUL

If you are looking for something likely to frighten you, you couldn't pick a better place to spend a Halloween night. West Town House is an abandoned great house not far from Dublin. It must have been a magnificent manor house at one time, but, like so many Irish houses, it was left to die of neglect. In the moist climate of Ireland this does not take very long. Many great houses have been left in this manner when land was gradually sold off from around them. The farmers buying the land have no interest in maintaining them. The great house remains aloof and alone, to die nobly and stand in ruins as mute witness of a bygone era in Irish history. The abandonment of the manor houses is the reaction to a romantic but unrealistic period in Irish life.

The way to get to West Town House is not simple, because it is easy to miss the entrance into the wilderness that surrounds the manor. Going north on the main Dublin-Belfast road, you exit just before the town of Naul. The estate is located about two miles off the road, beyond a modest gamekeeper's lodge. It seems completely neglected, even to the point that the road is hardly passable. About halfway toward the main house you have to abandon your car and walk.

Eventually you will find yourself in front of the great house with the

stable—now roofless—to the right. The three stories of the great house are completely windowless and even the floors have disappeared. The impression is that of a sightless giant blindly staring out into the landscape. Although the great house has been abandoned for many years, a lodge is maintained at the entrance to make sure that no poachers enter the game-rich estate.

You need no one's permission to go to West Town House. All you need is a keen sense of adventure and a good driver so that you don't miss the exit. It is wise, however, to leave five shillings as a token of respect with the doorkeeper.

A Dublin couple had wandered into the ruins not long ago. Both of them had felt a presence close enough to feel on their necks the breath of someone they could not see. Sybil Leek practically ran away from me when we set foot upon the shattered floor of the great house. In semitrance she relived a scene from Ireland's past. A group of people had met here, she explained,

people who were considered rebels in their day because they advocated the establishment of a parliamentary government in Ireland. This was the party that wanted the dail, or parliament, at a time when Ireland had not yet obtained her freedom from England. Apparently a young man by the name of Trehayne was among them. They had found him to have been a traitor and sentenced him to die. It was the restless spirit of the traitor Trehayne whom Sybil felt present in the ancient manor.

If you happen to be at West Town House and feel a presence—for Trehayne may very well still be there—be sure you don't discuss Irish politics. You can never tell how a ghost might react.

GERMANY

THE HAUNTED RUIN AT SCHWÄRZENBERG, BAVARIA

Schwärzenberg is an early medieval fortress, now largely in ruins, topping one of the hills between Regensburg and the Czechoslovakian border. It is due northeast of Regensburg, and it takes about an hour and a half to two hours on good country roads to reach it. Surrounded by parklike natural state forests, the area is extremely deserted and very beautiful. One can drive only to the foot of the hill upon which the fortress sits. One must walk the rest of the way, but the ascent is not difficult. The square towers of Schwärzenberg are still standing, and part of the halls are intact although the floors have all disappeared. Since the fortress has not been taken care of by the monument service, it is overgrown with various examples of the lush Bavarian flora, and rain and snow have partially filled the fortress with earth.

Those unable to drive up to the ruin can also reach it by railroad on a secondary line between Schwandorf and Fürth. The station to get off at is called Neubäu. From there one must either hire a car or walk for about two hours. No permission is needed to visit Schwärzenberg Fortress. There really isn't anyone there to give it. But it is best visited during the daytime. The forest paths leading up the hill are not easy to find in the dark of night, and there are absolutely no lights in the area.

Built around 1300, Schwärzenberg was destroyed twice. The first time

it was sacked during the Hussite Wars, when the Bohemian raiders came south to fight the Catholic armies of the emperor. This was in 1415 at the height of the first religious wars in Central Europe. In 1634, at the same time that the Swedes besieged Wolfsegg without success, they came to Schwärzenberg with considerable success. As a result of the Swedish destruction, Schwärzenberg is now only a ruin.

Legend has it that it is inhabited by a kind mountain spirit called Rotmantel or Redcoat.

Many years ago, Georg Rauchenberger, the owner of Wolfsegg Fortress, in the company of several friends, spent a night at Schwärzenberg. The purpose of the visit was to find out whether there was a ghost inhabiting the ancient ruin. On the first try nothing happened, but when they returned a second time, there was indeed something more than the noise of the surrounding forest or the animals running for shelter. In the middle of the night, they were all awakened by the sound of footsteps. It sounded to them as if a group of men was returning to the fortress, perhaps after a successful raid into the countryside. Schwärzenberg, like so many castles in the forests of Bavaria, was headquarters for robber-barons whose sole occupation was the pillaging of the countryside. While the group of observers lay still on the ground, the footsteps of long-dead, medieval soldiers could be clearly heard reverberating in the ruined halls of Schwärzenberg.

I brought Mrs. Edith Riedl to Schwärzenberg after our visit to Wolfsegg, and she was able to trace much of the violent history of this outpost.

Visibly shaken, she spoke of gangs of marauders coming from the fortress, spilling out into the countryside and returning later with much loot. She turned in horror from an area in the lower portion of the ruin, where the dungeons must have been located at one time. She still felt the impression of past cruelty and sufferings.

Even the conquering Swedes managed to imprint something of themselves upon the ruins. Mrs. Riedl vividly described the "foreigners" from the north who had come to destroy the fortress.

Schwärzenberg is not on any tourist map, but it is well worth a visit from the psychic point of view alone.

C. Buxheirden
'68

WOLFSEGG FORTRESS, BAVARIA

The fortified castle at Wolfsegg, Bavaria, is not state property and can be visited only through the kindness and permission of its owner. It is one of the few privately owned fortresses in the world, I believe, and thereby hangs a tale.

Georg Rauchenberger, by profession a painter and the official guardian of monuments for the province of The Upper Palatinate, which is part of the state of Bavaria, purchased this ancient fortress with his own savings. Since he is the man who passes on monies to be spent by the state for the restoration of ancient monuments in the province, he had of course a particularly touchy situation on his hands, for he could not possibly allow any funds to be diverted to his own castle. Consequently, every penny spent upon the restoration of this medieval fortress came from his own pocket. Over the years he has gradually restored this relic of the past into a livable, if primitive, medieval fortress. He has put in some of the missing wooden floors, and has turned the clock back to the eleventh century in every respect.

Two persons, so far, can sleep comfortably in the large fortress, but as it is still in the process of being restored, it will be a long time before it can compare with some of the "tourist attractions" under state control. Nevertheless, small groups of interested visitors have been admitted most days of the week for a guided tour through the Hall of Knights and other parts of the fortress. His charming niece, Xenia Huber, helps with visitors, since Mr. Rauchenberger works out of an office in Regensburg, a large city in Bavaria half an hour's drive away. Ordinarily visitors are not told of the hauntings at Wolfsegg, but I am sure that anyone referring to these lines will find at least a friendly reception. Arrangements for a visit to Wolfsegg must be made well in advance by writing to Georg Rauchenberger, care of Burg Wolfsegg bei Regensburg, Bavaria, Germany. A small donation is usually left with the guide taking people through the castle.

Because of the nearness of the River Danube, the fortress at Wolfsegg was always of some importance. It rises majestically out of the valley to the equivalent of four or five modern stories. Quite obviously constructed for defense, its thick bulky walls are forbidding, the small windows—high up to discourage aggressors—and the hill upon which the fortress perches making attack very difficult.

As a matter of fact, Wolfsegg never fell to an enemy, and even the formidable Swedes, who besieged it for a long time during the Thirty Years' War, had to give up. Built in 1028, Wolfsegg belonged to several noble Bavarian families and was always directly or indirectly involved in the intricate dynastic struggles between the various lines of the Wittelsbachs, who ruled Bavaria until 1918. Many of the masters of Wolfsegg made a living by being "Raubritter"—that is to say, robber barons. All in all, the area had an unsavory reputation even as early as the twelfth and thirteenth centuries. The walls are thick and the living quarters located well above ground.

The Knights Hall on the third floor is reached by a broad staircase, and one flight down there is also a lookout tower which has been restored as it was in the sixteenth century. In the inner court there is a wooden gallery running along part of the wall (at one time this gallery covered the entire length of the wall). The lower stories have not yet been fully restored or even explored.

Georg Rauchenberger himself has heard uncanny noises, footsteps, and experienced cold drafts at various times in various parts of the fortress. The late Mrs. Therese Pielmeier, wife of the custodian, actually saw a whitish form in the yard, full of luminescence, and she also heard various unexplained noises. On one occasion, Mr. Rauchenberger saw a young lady coming in with a small group of visitors, and when he turned to speak to her she disappeared.

I held a séance at Wolfsegg with a Viennese lady who served as my medium at the time. Through the trance mediumship of Mrs. Edith Riedl, I was able to trace the terrible story of a triple murder involving a beautiful woman, once the wife of a Wolfsegg baron, who had become the innocent

victim of a political plot. The legend of the beautiful ghost at Wolfsegg had, of course, existed prior to our arrival on the scene. Apparently, greedy relatives of a fourteenth-century owner of Wolfsegg had decided to take over the property, then of considerable value, by trapping the young wife of the owner with another man. The husband, told of the rendezvous, arrived in time to see the two lovers together, killed both of them, and was in turn murdered in "just revenge" by his cunning relatives.

The portrait of the unlucky lady of Wolfsegg hangs in one of the corridors, the work of the father of the current owner, who painted her from impressions received while visiting the castle.

Although I was able to make contact with the atmosphere surrounding the "white woman" of Wolfsegg, and to shed light upon a hitherto unknown Renaissance tragedy, it is entirely possible that the restless baroness still roams the corridors to find recognition and to prove her innocence to the world.

One reaches Wolfsegg on secondary roads in about a half hour's drive from Regensburg, and it is situated near a small and rather primitive village, northwest of the city on the north side of the Danube River. There is only one inn in this village, and staying overnight, as I once did, is not recommended.

This is a remote and strange area of Germany, despite the comparative nearness of the city of Regensburg. By the way Regensburg is sometimes also called Ratisbon, and is the center of one of the few remaining strongly Celtic areas in Germany.

AUSTRIA

SCHLOSS ALTENBERG, STYRIA

Schloss Altenberg is situated at the little village of Hitzendorf, near Graz, capital of the province of Styria, Austria. It can be reached by car in less than half an hour from Graz, and is at present operated as a small guest house where one can stay overnight and have breakfast and dinner. The appointments are very simple, and consequently inexpensive, and advance reservations are imperative since Altenberg cannot cope with more than three or four guests at a time.

The lady who manages the castle for its owner, an attorney in Vienna, is extremely understanding when it comes to ghosts. She herself has had her share of experiences in the castle, and some of the servants have also. I can vouch for the authenticity of the hauntings myself, for when my wife and I stayed there three years ago, we knew nothing whatsoever about any hauntings, yet experienced things that we did not expect.

Altenberg consists of two main stories and a roofed attic. Various turrets jut out from the roof, giving it rather a storybook castle appearance. Around it there are old trees and a lovely garden. Behind the castle itself lies a farm, which in olden times supplied the necessities for the owners of the castle. Today the farm is subleased to a professional farmer and is no longer connected with the castle.

Some of the reception rooms on the second floor have been turned into guest rooms, and one in particular, looking rather like a chamber for judicial procedures, was the center for our psychic experience. I had the distinct impression of a man in the livery of a bygone age standing in the general vicinity of a large closet and peering at me from sad and rather hollow eyes. The following morning I learned that the closet actually hid a door behind which a corridor led to the outside. As for the man in the old livery, there too was a basis in fact.

In the early nineteenth century, one of the owners of the castle had come to be on very bad terms with his farmers. When his oppressive tactics aroused them to open rebellion, they searched for him in order to kill him. His valet helped him hide in the area of the closet. The rebels could not find the owner of the castle and were therefore thwarted in their efforts to kill him. The valet later betrayed him to the rebels and saw him killed before his very eyes. His remorseful ghost apparently still finds itself drawn to the area of his crime.

But that was not the only psychic impression we had that night. My wife also felt herself overcome with strong religious feelings as soon as she had lain down in the ornate bed assigned to her. She felt strong emanations

of an unseen presence connected with the bed, but found them neither upsetting nor threatening in any way. Next morning I discovered that the bed
my wife had used had belonged to a bishop.

If you wish to venture into this area of Austria—which is far off the
beaten track as far as tourism goes—you will find Altenberg a charming inter-
lude, whether or not you encounter the ghostly valet or sleep in the bishop's
bed.

ERNEGG CASTLE

Among the unusual and little-known attractions of Austria are some of the privately owned castles nowadays taking guests for a night or two. The appointments in most of these places are generally simple, if not primitive, but what the places lack in Hilton-type comforts they more than make up for in romantic atmosphere and sometimes ghostly legends.

Ernegg lies on a country road leading south from the Danube. One leaves on the main road from Vienna and drives in the direction of Ybbs, the nearest large town. Ernegg is about two hours' drive from Vienna, and is clearly visible from a distance as one approaches.

The castle belongs to the Princes Auersberg, and it is now operated as a pension where one can stay a day or a week with the calm surroundings of the countryside and the forest as prime attractions. The food is simple and good; the prices are very modest; and the lady manager speaks excellent English. Those wishing to visit Ernegg need only address themselves to Mrs. H. Lee, Direktor, Schloss Ernegg bei Ybbs, Oberösterreich, or Upper Austria, Austria. Most of the guests at Ernegg are local people from some of the central Austrian cities, or a few Viennese who like unusual or out of the way places.

Ernegg Castle sits on a hill looking down into the valley and toward the small town of Stein am Forst. It is an imposing Renaissance structure built of white stone in a style reminiscent of northern Italian castles. There are three stories and an inner courtyard of pergolas or round arches allowing one to walk even if it is raining. The many arches of this courtyard give the building a certain elegance, even though the rooms themselves are generally simple. All rooms are individually heated by the peculiarly Austrian, tall tile-covered stoves which must be filled early in the morning and again late at night to provide the necessary heat.

The main area of the alleged haunting of Ernegg is to be found in what is now the apartment of the owners. However, even this part of the castle is available to guests during certain parts of the year when the owners are away. It is best to ask the director for the rooms where the ghostly lovers allegedly

have been seen. The story goes that a young man was courting one of the Auersberg daughters. Since he was only a servant in the castle, Prince Auersberg disapproved. On one such occasion the young man was found in a part of the castle where he had no business to be, and was consequently arrested. In the manner of the late Middle Ages, he was summarily executed by the castle owner who had full jurisdiction over all those who lived under his roof. The ghost of this unfortunate groom is said to haunt that part of the castle now used by the family itself.

Whether or not a sensitive visitor will pick up this imprint from the past, or perhaps some other impression, is anyone's guess, but Ernegg definitely warrants a visit.

THE HAUNTED DUNGEON, STEYERSBERG

Steyersberg Castle is a sprawling, imposing group of sixteenth- and seventeenth-century buildings. It is a romantic castle, sitting atop a hill, surrounded by tall trees, looking out on the Austrian mountains, isolated from modern life even though it is only an hour and a half from Vienna by car. The castle was rebuilt, as far as conveniences are concerned, by the late Count Degenhard von Wurmbrand, whose family has owned it for centuries.

There are sixty rooms and forty bathrooms in the castle now, and many of them are extremely comfortable—far more than one could expect in a building of this age. It is privately owned and visitors are not encouraged. The heirs of Count Wurmbrand who own the castle now, may make an exception now and again for someone coming from afar. If arrangements are made well in advance, a visit might be possible. The late count's sister Henrietta Countess Kolowrat still resides at Steyersberg. The post office is at Warth, Niederösterreich, or Lower Austria.

It is in the oldest part of the castle that the hauntings have been observed. The dungeon, reaching great depths and built directly into the rock itself, was the scene of innumerable hardships from the Middle Ages onward. In particular, it appears that in the seventeenth century a distant relative of the last Count Wurmbrand had imprisoned three men in the dungeon on

trumped-up charges. In those days there was no other justice than the justice of the lord of the castle, consequently the men were left to die in their prison. One of them, so the story goes, managed to curse the Wurmbrand family before his death. Because of the wrong done him and his friends, no male member of the Wurmbrands should ever die naturally until such time as the last male heir bearing the Wurmbrand name had died.

Although the branch of the family which was cursed was only distantly related to the Count Wurmbrand I knew, the curse eventually also applied to him.

While I was still trying to arrange for a séance to break the ancient curse, Count Wurmbrand was taken to a local hospital for a minor complaint. By a strange set of circumstances, he suffered a hemorrhage while in the hospital. This happened at a time when no doctor could be found immediately, and precious minutes passed. By the time some help came, it was too late. When Degenhard von Wurmbrand died a few years ago, the last male to bear that name was gone. The curse had taken its toll.

That fact does not necessarily mean that the area around and above the dungeon is now free from psychic activities. Others also died there tragically.

Prior to meeting me, the last Count Wurmbrand experienced a vision in which he saw three blackbirds appear before him, which he felt were the three unfortunate prisoners from the dungeon. Cold, clammy feelings touch anyone walking through the apartment directly above the dungeon, which has long been walled up.

Anyone wishing to buy a haunted castle that really looks the way a castle looks at Disneyland might give Steyersberg a thought. Although it is not exactly on the market, the castle is much too large for the present owners. Of course, castles no longer come cheap in Austria, ghosts or no ghosts. But so long as the new owner is not a blood relative of the von Wurmbrands, he is reasonably safe.

IMPERIAL CASTLE, VIENNA

The majority of tourists visiting the Imperial Castle in Vienna are shown the sumptuous reception rooms, the state rooms, the treasuries, both worldly and religious, but never the haunted areas of the castle. It remained for me to rediscover these areas much to the amazement of the castle officials themselves. They had never been told of the haunted areas.

The castle was the ancient seat of Austria's emperors, and before that of the Holy Roman Emperors. The building goes back to the beginning of the Middle Ages, but there are many additions. The major portion of the "Old Castle" of Vienna came into existence after 1400. The thirteenth and four-teenth century wing is called "Schweizerhof," or Swiss Court.

Walking up to the second floor of this "tract," or portion of the castle, one finds oneself in an area where the walls are two to three yards thick. Here was a small monastery of the Capuchin friars, for the personal use of members of the Imperial family only. Later this monastery was discontinued and the area became part of the castle. But a ghostly monk has been seen in the area from time to time, walking the dark corridors connecting this ancient portion of the castle with the more modern sections.

A short walk from the Capuchin monastery area of the castle lies a sec-tion I have written about and which is connected with the tragedy of Crown

Prince Rudolf and his love Mary Vetsera. The story of the Mayerling lovers and their alleged suicide, or—in my opinion—double murder I have reported in *Window to the Past*. It is an historical fact that Rudolf and Mary met at the Imperial Castle time and again. There is a staircase leading up from the first to the second floor, which Mary must have used to gain access to Rudolf's apartment. After the tragedy, in the late 1880s, the stairwell nearby was walled up, the door nailed shut, and a heavy closet moved against it to cover any trace of a connecting link between the two floors at this point. Between the two staircases lies the area where the whitish figure of a woman has been observed by a number of witnesses. This figure appeared shortly after the tragedy at Mayerling. Apparently, the figure comes up the stairs from the lower floor, glides along the corridor, and then disappears toward Rudolf's apartment.

It is not surprising that Mary should still be attracted to this part of the Imperial Castle, where she lived through some of her happiest moments. Mayerling held only tragedy for her.

The Imperial Castle is always available to tourists, but in order to see the areas just described it is perhaps wisest to ask for permission or at least for a guide to come along. One addresses oneself to the administrator of the castle, or "Burghauptmann."

At the spot where the stairs reaches the corridor there is now a "marterl", a peculiarly Austrian madonna encased in glass and meant to be a miniature shrine for those who wish to pray en route to their destination. Why the holy picture was placed at this particular point no one seems to know, but it seems of relatively recent origin and may well be linked up with the tragedy of Mary Vetsera.

Those who wish to visit Mayerling as well can of course do so. One of the photographs taken by me at Mayerling does show a ghostly presence. It is male and may well link up with the death of Crown Prince Rudolf. Whether it is the unhappy prince himself, or perhaps one of his remorseful murderers, or someone else, is not clear. At any rate, Mayerling is now a Carmelite monastery and can be reached by road in about half an hour from Vienna. It can be visited freely, although there is no one to take one behind the principal chapel. This is hardly necessary, since the chapel represents the very heart of the tragedy. Prior to being turned into a chapel, the area was divided into two floors, the lower being the reception hall of what was then a hunting lodge, with the upper story having been the bedroom in which the two lovers died. The Emperor Franz Joseph, upon hearing the terrible news, ordered the transformation of his son's hunting lodge into a strict Carmelite monastery.

ITALY

CASTLE ROVINA, MERANO

Merano is a bustling town in the resort area of the Italian Tyrol. It has a large number of hotels, some industry, and a number of "castles." The latter are simply the ancestral seats of the various noble families in the area. Anyone simply asking for "The Castle" in Merano may have trouble locating the right one. There is, first of all, the Castle Tyrol, outside the city proper. Located on a hill overlooking the Merano Valley, Castle Tyrol gave the country its name. Here the counts of Tyrol resided during the Middle Ages. Today, a small village surrounds the castle, and the village is also called Tyrol.

One of the best preserved castles in "downtown" Merano is the Castle Rovina. Merano is largely German speaking and the Austrian name for Rovina is Ruben. The castle has been privately owned for centuries and still is. The family of the counts du Parc has a long record in Imperial Austrian service, although originally of French origin. A few years ago the family decided to take in a few paying guests to help defray the upkeep of the large castle. There are accommodations for about ten people, offering bed and breakfast.

My wife, Catherine, was born at this castle. During World War II the du Parc family shared the castle with my wife's family. It was then that she

experienced certain psychic phenomena, such as chills, uncanny feelings, footsteps, and my late brother-in-law Count Fédor Buxhoeveden, who was then a little boy, reported that he saw a whitish hand reach out of nowhere and pull the cover off his bed. My wife's family then lived in the oldest part of the castle.

The castle itself has three stories and a tower which today contains the private apartment of the aging count du Parc. The rooms available to visitors face toward the valley and the city of Merano, and there is a lovely porch opening onto the lush garden below. Although Castle Rovina is actually in the middle of town, the feeling of being in the country is very strong. It is surrounded by a large and very green garden with ancient trees.

In another part of the castle there is a chapel, dating back to the early Middle Ages, although most of it stems from the Renaissance period. Castle Rovina is surrounded by a thick gray wall, and it is easily reached from downtown Merano in five minutes. One then drives along a carefully kept driveway into the courtyard of the castle. Merano itself can be reached by railroad or car from both Austria and Italy, and the nearest airport is at Bolzano.

I have no idea who the ghost at Rovina is. For obvious personal reasons, it was not possible to bring a psychic to the castle. Thus, anyone reading these lines who wishes to find out whether or not Rovina has a resident ghost can do so in virgin territory. But he should be warned that the family does not like to discuss the matter, and anyone asking for accommodations and stressing the ghostly aspects might not be welcome. On the other hand, a quiet and well-behaved visitor interested in ancient castles, wishing to spend a night or two at Castle Rovina, could find such an experience rewarding in many ways.

One addresses oneself to the Countess du Parc, Castle Rovina, Merano, Italy.